A COMPREHENSIVE GUIDE TO MASTERING ADULT ADHD

KEY QUESTIONS AND ANSWERS TO

Understanding Therapeutic and Non-therapeutic Options to Enhance your Focus, Navigate Your Emotions, Break Through Barriers and Live Boldly

Vivian Boma Abobo. PharmD.MBA

Table of Contents

INTRODUCTION 1

ABOUT THE AUTHOR 2

CHAPTER 1: WHAT IS ADULT ADHD? 5

ATTENTION DEFICIT HYPERACTIVITY DISORDER 5

STATISTICS OF ADHD 6

    ADHD Prevalence in Children 6

    ADHD Prevalence in Adults 7

CONSEQUENCES OF ADHD IN ADULTS 8

SEVERITY OF ADHD 9

    Mild ADHD 10

    Moderate ADHD 10

    Severe ADHD 10

CHAPTER 2: HOW IS ADHD DIAGNOSED? 13

SIGNS AND SYMPTOMS OF ADHD 14

    Attention-Deficit 15

    Hyperactivity and Impulsivity 17

    Mixed 18

PREVALENCE 18

DIAGNOSIS 19

CHAPTER 3: CAN ADULT ADHD BE CURED? 23

WHAT IS NEURODIVERSITY? 23

OTHER NEURODIVERGENT CONDITIONS 26

    Autism 27

    Learning Disabilities 28

UNTREATED ADULT ADHD 29

**CHAPTER 4: WHAT CONDITIONS ARE COMORBID WITH ADULT
ADHD?** 31

DEPRESSION 31
    ADHD and Depression Treatment 35
ANXIETY 38
    Does ADHD Make Anxiety Worse? 40
    Treatment of ADHD and Anxiety 41
    Other Coping Mechanisms for ADHD and Anxiety Today 42
SUBSTANCE USE DISORDER 44
    Why Do Adults with ADHD Develop SUD? 44
    Are Stimulant Drugs for ADHD Addictive? 46
    Treatment for ADHD with Substance Use Disorder 49
    Addiction and ADHD Medication 50
    Reaching Out for Help 51

CHAPTER 5: WHAT COPING MECHANISMS CAN I USE TO MANAGE SYMPTOMS OF ADULT ADHD? 53

CREATING TO-DO LISTS 54
JOURNALING 55
MEDITATING 56
WATCHING YOUR BUDGET 56
EXERCISING 57
KEEPING TRACK OF YOUR STRENGTHS 58
PLAYING BRAIN GAMES 58
OUTSOURCING 59
SLEEPING 60

CHAPTER 6: WHAT NON-PHARMACEUTICAL TREATMENT OPTIONS ARE AVAILABLE FOR ADULT ADHD? 63

BEHAVIOR MANAGEMENT INTERVENTIONS 64
    Contingency Management 66
    Benefits of Behavior Management Interventions 69
PHYSIOLOGICAL TREATMENTS 70
    Physical Exercise 70
    Weekly Exercise Routine 74
    Diet 76
COGNITIVE BEHAVIORAL THERAPY 83
    Benefits of CBT for Adults with ADHD 84
    CBT and Results 87
    How Effective Is CBT? 87

CHAPTER 7: WHAT PHARMACEUTICAL TREATMENT OPTIONS ARE AVAILABLE FOR ADULT ADHD? 89

COMMON ADHD MEDICATION 90
    Stimulant Therapies 90
    Non-Stimulants 96
ANTIDEPRESSANT MEDICATION OPTIONS FOR ADHD 98
BENEFITS OF ADHD MEDICATIONS 99
POSSIBLE SIDE EFFECTS 102
INTERACTIONS WITH OTHER MEDICATIONS 108

CHAPTER 8: WHAT SUBSTANCES INTERACT WITH MY ADHD MEDICATIONS? 111

ALCOHOL INTERACTION WITH ADHD MEDICATION 113
ANTIDEPRESSANTS INTERACTION WITH ADHD MEDICATION 114
CAFFEINE INTERACTION WITH ADHD MEDICATION 116
VITAMIN C 119
OTHER SUBSTANCES 121

CHAPTER 9: CAN I CONTINUE TO WORK AFTER MY ADHD DIAGNOSIS? 123

ADHD IN WORK SETTINGS 123
    Inattentiveness 124
    Poor Organization Skills 126
    Procrastination 127
    Poor Communication Skills 128
    Sluggish Cognitive Tempo 129
    Lethargic Behavior 130
    Daydreaming 133
    Slowness in Processing Information 133
    Time Myopia 134
    Executive Dysfunction 135
    Should You Tell Your Employer About Your ADHD Diagnosis? 137
EXAMPLES OF SUCCESSFUL ADHDERS 140

CHAPTER 10: CAN I DRIVE AND OPERATE MACHINERY WITH ADULT ADHD? 142

SAFE DRIVING ADVICE FOR PEOPLE LIVING WITH ADHD 146

CHAPTER 11: WHERE CAN I FIND SUPPORT AND RESOURCES FOR MY ADULT ADHD? 148

SUPPORT FOR ADULT ADHD 148
    Partner Support 149
    Parent Support 153
    Workplace Support 155
RESOURCES FOR ADULT ADHD 158
    Non-Profit Organizations 158
    Blogs 163
    Online Communities 164
    Books 166

CHAPTER 12: LIST OF COMMON ADHD MEDICATIONS 170

CONCLUSION 176

REFERENCES

Introduction

There are several books out there—books about ADHD and mental health, books about neurodivergence and stigmatization—there are books that have changed the lives of those living with ADHD, but they are not enough. When you or someone you know gets an ADHD diagnosis, they will need all the information they can get, and that is where the problem seeps in; where can people find reliable information about adult ADHD? Is there enough research? Do they have access to books? Are they reading reviewed content? The list goes on and on, but some readers stumble upon knowledge gems that help them throughout the journey. *Adult ADHD* is one such treasure.

In this book, you will learn to reframe your mindset around ADHD so you can view the diagnosis as an identity, rather than an illness or a curse of some sort. This book also teaches about neurodiversity as a valid way of being and offers some helpful advice on how one can thrive in a neurotypical society.

Readers often complain about out-of-date statistics when they read some old books, but that also happens with new books that just do not have as thorough research as one would expect. With that in mind, this guide includes data and information from recent studies.

In *Adult ADHD*, you will also discover that the condition is not a handicap. While its symptoms can be debilitating, this manuscript maintains a positive attitude toward and recognizes ADHD as an identity, so you can approach your condition with compassion. This book is for adults who were diagnosed with ADHD, their relatives, close friends, or any other curious minds looking to learn some essential facts when living with ADHD. Adult ADHD seeks to validate readers and lead them as they learn to develop coping mechanisms. It will also help them find treatment options that best fit their needs so they may increase their efficiency at work and build better relationships with their loved ones.

About the Author

Dr. V.B ABOBO has a doctorate degree in pharmacy and has been in the medical and pharmaceutical industries for more than 20 years. With her in-depth knowledge about psychiatric disorders and treatment options available, the author has sat in several medical rounds involving patient care to make recommendations on therapeutic management of their problems.

The author has had exposure to adults with ADHD who had difficulties concentrating and others who lost their jobs and loved ones due to a lack of understanding of their pathology or disease. After seeing the suffering that can arise from lacking reliable information about the condition, she decided to share her knowledge so people living with ADHD may take control of their situations and achieve success at work and in their relationships.

Apart from the author's passion for helping those who have ADHD, she also feels her educational background and experience make it her duty to ensure everyone diagnosed with adult ADHD receives enough education about it. This helps the readers discover answers to some of the critical questions they and their loved ones may have.

Dr. V.B ABOBO has also served in different capacities, including management and clinical roles, to recommend appropriate drug therapy to the medical staff while placing emphasis on patient safety and efficacy. That includes her service as a member of the council of pharmacy executives at Texas Medical Center. The author has numerous publications with the American Society of Health System Pharmacists and has co-authored publications with the American Journal of Psychiatry and the Drug Information Association (DIA). She was nominated for the President's Award for Mentoring Women at the University of Texas. Her other awards include Nominee for Diamond Manager of the Year at the University of Texas, Roche Preceptor of the Year, and Winner of Clinical Excellence Award with McKesson Medication Management.

"Dear reader, I am so happy you decided to purchase my book despite all the different options you had. I authored this book because of my passion as a pharmacist to help families dealing with varying illnesses and to make recommendations about pharmacotherapy and treatment options," says Dr. V.B. ABOBO.

Chapter 1:

What is Adult ADHD?

Focusing on important issues seems easy for other people, but I am not good at this!

When you have *ADHD*, your life may feel different because of how the people around you do things you cannot or how they *do not* do the things you do. It gets worse when those in your life do not know you suffer from *ADHD* and think whatever is going on with you is a block you should work on breaking or that you *just* lack self-control.

People living with undiagnosed *ADHD* deal with various kinds of problems, from being misunderstood to being ridiculed, especially if they find out when they are already grown. It can make your love complicated, but if you devote some of your time to finding ways to move forward, you can live happily with *ADHD*.

Attention Deficit Hyperactivity Disorder

Attention Deficit Hyperactivity Disorder (ADHD) is a neurodevelopmental disorder characterized by a combination of symptoms that show inattentiveness, hyperactivity, or impulsivity. We will discuss more on the symptoms of ADHD in the next chapter, but first, it is important that you understand its statistics and severity.

Statistics of ADHD

If you or someone you know has just discovered they have ADHD, you may be curious to know how common it is as well as what kind of people are most likely to have it. In this section, we will focus on that and various other questions you might have.

ADHD Prevalence in Children

Although the approximate statistics of ADHD diagnosis vary from region to region, millions of children in the United States have been diagnosed with ADHD, making it one of the most prevalent neurodevelopmental disorders in children (Centers for Disease Control and Prevention, 2021) and (National Institute of Mental Health, n.d.).

Statistics also show that female children are less likely to be diagnosed with ADHD as compared to male kids. Hispanic or Asian, non-Hispanic children are the least commonly diagnosed with ADHD, followed by White children who are non-Hispanic. The most diagnosed children are those of Black, non-Hispanic ancestry (Centers for Disease Control and Prevention, 2021).

In most instances, children who have ADHD also suffer from other mental, behavioral, or emotional problems such as anxiety, *autism spectrum disorder*, and depression. However, contrary to what some people think about ADHD, the mental issue does not only affect children. The scientific evidence that ADHD persists into adulthood brings us to our next section— the entire point of the book.

ADHD Prevalence in Adults

A 2016 study estimated a 2.8% prevalence rate for adult ADHD throughout the world, and the rates of diagnosis are soaring (ADDitude Editors, 2006), (Chung et al., 2019) and (Fayyad et al., 2016).

Getting a diagnosis of ADHD at 25 may make one feel better because then they will know something is wrong and they are not "just lazy", but it can also be terrible. It can be difficult to accept all the years that passed when one was in the dark about their mental state, trying things and failing. Realizing later in life can feel so different from carrying ADHD into adulthood that one may find themselves wondering why they were not diagnosed earlier.

There are several reasons that may cause individuals not to know they have ADHD until later in life. Some of these factors may include stigmatization, fear of medication, good coping skills, and misdiagnosis. The way some people judge those with ADHD can discourage others from taking the necessary steps toward getting proper diagnoses. This causes them to endure ADHD symptoms for as long as they can. When the yoke of uncertainty becomes too heavy, that is when they make the visit to their physicians and receive a diagnosis after years of wondering. Those who have great coping abilities unintentionally mask their symptoms, and those who fear receiving medication may purposefully avoid getting the diagnosis, so they do not have to take any drugs. The symptoms of ADHD may be a little different in adults, but they often become more difficult to cope with as the demands of adult life. Increases eventually, they are diagnosed late.

Consequences of ADHD in Adults

Adults who have ADHD are more likely to have a lower quality of life, especially if the condition is left untreated. This is because it often interferes with day-to-day life and makes it challenging for the individuals who have it to carry on with normal lives.

People with ADHD may even have trouble finding and keeping employment more than adults who do not have it. This is especially true for those who, for one reason or another, did not receive treatment for their ADHD while they were children. The professional world may be unforgiving when one has trouble paying attention or waiting their turn and displaying such behavior may look like one does not have control of their life.

Individuals who suffer from ADHD are also prone to have issues in all forms of relationships because those around them may have trouble understanding them.

Because there is only so much one can handle, these individuals are at an increased risk of developing bad habits, anxiety, and mood problems, as well as challenges with tasks that require focus, such as driving.

When compared to males with ADHD and women who do not have it, the prevalence of poor self-esteem in women who have ADHD is significantly higher. All the external criticism they receive may make them lose confidence and withdraw. Females with ADHD are also less likely to take medication for their condition than men living with the same condition.

However, it is important to know that receiving an ADHD diagnosis is not the end, but a step closer to reclaiming control over your life and relations. There are plenty of ways to help you cope with the condition without the fear of being judged, and we will soon get to that.

Severity of ADHD

ADHD has varying degrees of severity, so some people exhibit mild symptoms while others have had their lives significantly impacted by the condition to an extent that it is difficult to continue living as usual. Some individuals with serious ADHD struggle with substance misuse and others are unable to maintain employment.

Because the symptoms of ADHD can manifest themselves differently in different individuals, when professionals diagnose it, the DSM-5 requires them to be categorized as mild, moderate, or severe to indicate the degree of impairment associated with the symptoms. The severity of the condition may change depending on how it manifests over the course of one's life. If one's presentation worsens after they have already got a mild, their mental healthcare provider reassesses them and classifies the severity as appropriate.

Mild ADHD

Mild, means that the individual in question presents with a few symptoms of ADHD, but not enough for the mental healthcare provider to make a diagnosis. Cases of mild ADHD have symptoms that cause only a slight amount of impairment in the person's academic, social, and professional lives.

Moderate ADHD

Moderate ADHD is the gray shade of the condition. It has symptoms that lie between mild and severe.

Severe ADHD

Severe means that the person has many symptoms, and they exceed the number required to give a diagnosis. In instances of severe ADHD, the individual shows several severe symptoms. You may also find that the symptoms have an obvious negative impact on the person's work, school, business, or social life.

Treatment strategies vary depending on the severity of one's symptoms and may change to suit the situation.

Chapter 2:

How is ADHD Diagnosed?

ADHD stands for attention deficit hyperactivity disorder. It is described as a disorder that develops over the course of a person's lifetime and starts in childhood but can continue into adulthood. This condition has an impact not just on how a person acts, but also on how their brain processes information and carries out its functions. In the past, attention deficit hyperactivity disorder (ADHD) was thought of as a condition that only affected children. However, recent research has shown that the effects of ADHD can also cause different behavioral changes in adults. As a result, a significant amount of emphasis needs to be placed on both children and adults so that ADHD can be diagnosed at an early stage and appropriate health services can be provided on time. There has been a lot of research done, and it has helped narrow down some risk factors that can lead to neurological impairment, which can then lead to this illness. However, the specific reason for this behavior pattern is not yet understood, but it has helped limit some risk factors. It is vital to notice the symptoms of ADHD and make a diagnosis in both children and adults to lessen the influence that this condition can have on the individual's typical behavioral development. The symptoms of ADHD can have a significant impact on a person's day-to-day life, including their character development, capacity to interact with others, and ability to do things with the level of efficiency that is expected of them. It is essential to keep in mind that adults, in addition to children, can be impacted by ADHD to the same degree, and because of this, both groups need to be given the utmost care.

Signs and Symptoms of ADHD

The indications and symptoms of ADHD in children and adults are varied and include changes in behavioral characteristics that have a detrimental impact on the person's life. It is essential to understand the fact that the signs and symptoms of ADHD in adults are not as clearly defined as they are in children. This is because most of the studies that have been conducted and documented have mostly focused on children. However, this does not negate the fact that ADHD is becoming more prevalent in adults; hence, we cannot ignore the possibility of this illness occurring in adults.

As we go over the signs and symptoms of ADHD in children and adults, it is essential to keep in mind that not all people who have ADHD present the same or have the same symptoms. As a result, a caregiver must treat each person presenting with ADHD on an individual basis with compassion and understanding. To facilitate a more complete comprehension of the indications and symptoms, they have been organized into the following three categories:

Attention-Deficit

Attention deficit simply means lack of attention. This can present itself in a person's lack of concentration and focus to carry out duties, lack of interest in socializing and education, which manifests as scholastic challenges, and lack of motivation to learn new things, which manifests as a lack of motivation to learn new things.

In Children

Children that suffer from this condition typically have difficulty concentrating on their tasks , which means that they are easily sidetracked . It is said that they have deficient performance in their schoolwork and that they have trouble creating and maintaining relationships with others. Children who have attention deficit hyperactivity disorder (ADHD) are often described as children who want to avoid activities that require complete concentration because they are slow in paying attention and have poor listening abilities. Children who have ADHD are typically forgetful and have poor organizational abilities, making it difficult for them to store things in an order that is suitable for their age. Carelessness, which may manifest itself either at school or in the tasks that are assigned, is another indicator and symptom. They moreover have the propensity to lose stuff without justification, such as school task resources (books, pencils, rubbers, etc.).

In Adults

ADHD in adults begins in infancy or youth, although the condition often is not recognized until much later in life. The signs and symptoms of ADHD in adults are less obvious than they are in youngsters. An adult who suffers from adult deficit hyperactivity disorder has difficulty maintaining their concentration. They struggle to get projects off the ground or see them through to completion, and they are typically terrible at sticking to schedules. They are either terrible at staying organized or forgetful, and they pay no attention to the smallest of details. Some persons who have ADHD are known to engage in substance misuse because they turn to the usage of recreational drugs to maintain their level of concentration. A significant number of persons who have ADHD take these newly developed medications to treat and get a handle on the three symptoms. It has also been demonstrated that adults who suffer from ADHD have low self-esteem; in fact, they typically exhibit a lack of esteem and have poor interaction skills with other people, including members of their families, their friends, and their social connections. This has a significant impact on the activities and performance they engage in on a day-to-day basis. For instance, due to their inability to focus and concentrate, people with ADHD tend to have poor academic performance, which is reflected in their bad grades. Additional signs and symptoms include but are not limited to procrastination, hopelessness, frustration, risk-taking, anxiety, involvement in criminal activities, and so on.

Hyperactivity and Impulsivity

Those who fit under this group are known to be impulsive or hyperactive. They have serious impulse control issues. This is because they typically give the impression of being extremely chatty, unpleasant, and are frequently described as having uncontrollable restlessness. They may display signs of being overly active or out of control, such as:

- Fidgeting often.

- Displaying improper behaviors such as running up and down excessively.

- Easily getting mad and acting before thinking about the consequences.

- Being uncomfortable in one position.

Many ADHDers have a poor tolerance for frustration. They are quick to get angry over minor issues and are more likely to have troubled marriages and greater rates of divorce when compared to the general population.

People with ADHD may also be a source of distraction for those around them. This means they often struggle to enjoy leisure activities on their own because they may want to continuously involve or interrupt others who may be busy with their own activities. Some individuals who have ADHD also have trouble waiting. If they are having a conversation with other people, they may interrupt often, sometimes even before understanding what the other person was going to say.

This habit can also show itself in adults as a feeling of restlessness when they are not interested in anything. They have the propensity to respond rapidly in response to a scenario without giving additional attention to the potential risks it may bring, which means they tend to make hasty decisions without considering the potential repercussions of their actions. An illustration of this might be participating in risky sports, making rash decisions at work, driving recklessly, or making other significant choices in life without giving them enough thought. It might be challenging for adults who have hyperactive or impulsive conduct to maintain control over their feelings.

Mixed

A person can be mixed if they have both attention deficit and hyperactivity/impulsive disorder and present with signs of both disorders. It is possible that certain symptoms will become more noticeable during childhood, while others will do so during adulthood. For instance, the signs and symptoms are typically more noticeable in youngsters, but they may only appear in adults in the form of irritability and difficulty making decisions (impulsiveness).

Prevalence

It is estimated that between 15 and 20 percent of the total population of youngsters suffer from ADHD. It has been stated that more boys than girls are affected by the prevalence of the condition.

It has been estimated that between 2 and 7 percent of the overall population is affected by ADHD in adults, with reports claiming an equal distribution between males and females who have been impacted.

It has been observed that the prevalence of ADHD in adults is higher in those who abuse substances, and it has also been stated that people who abuse substances have a worse prognosis and a higher likelihood of relapsing after receiving treatment.

Diagnosis

Certified medical professionals who have been educated to recognize and treat diseases of this nature are the ones who are qualified to make the diagnosis of ADHD. The Diagnostic and Statistical Manual of Mental Disorders, Fifth Edition (DSM-5) published by the American Association of Psychiatry is used to determine a diagnosis of Attention Deficit Hyperactivity Disorder (ADHD). The diagnosis is arrived at by analyzing the symptoms that a person has presented with, considering both the length of time that the symptoms have been present and the influence that they have had on the individual's day-to-day life. The assessment will consist of gathering information about the patient's history from the patient's family, making a note of the age at which the first symptoms appeared, the behavioral pattern, observing the patient, and reviewing the child's school reports to determine how well the child is doing in school. Following this, the patient will be evaluated, and various medical tests will be performed, to eliminate the possibility of other medical or psychiatric diseases, such as mood or anxiety disorders.

For the DSM-5 diagnosis to be considered accurate, each of the following criteria must be met. In children younger than 17 years old, there should be a presence of six or more symptoms of attention deficit or hyperactivity or a combination of symptoms.

The signs must have been noticed in two or more locations, such as a household, a school, or a church, and the symptoms must have persisted for a minimum of six months or longer. The presence of at least five of the symptoms described earlier enables a diagnosis to be made in an adult who is older than 17 years of age.

There should be proof that the symptoms have had a detrimental influence on the person's life in some way, whether socially, mentally, intellectually, or in some other way. The criteria established by the ASRS can also be used to arrive at a diagnosis of ADHD.

ASRS is an abbreviation for the adult self-report scale. It is a diagnostic instrument that consists of questions that are used to diagnose and evaluate the symptoms of ADHD in individuals who are older than 18 years old. The Adult self-report scale questionnaire was developed by the World Health Organization and consists of eighteen questions. These questions assist evaluate a person's behavior over the past six months by providing information on how they have been behaving on the Adult self-report scale. This is a self-reporting method that the patient is responsible for completing, and its criteria are in relation to and reference the Diagnostic and Statistical Manual of Mental Disorders, Fifth Edition (DSM-5). It is helpful in doing in-depth research and gaining knowledge of a person's capacity to carry out specific duties, such as managing time effectively, being organized, evaluating restlessness, and so on.

The questionnaire is broken up into two parts, referred to respectively as part A and part B. It is requested that the patient who is presenting themselves or the person fills out the questions in parts A and B by checking the boxes that most accurately represent or reflect the manifestation of their symptoms. There are six questions in Part A, and they serve as a screening tool to identify the signs and symptoms of attention deficit hyperactivity disorder in adults. If a diagnosis is made based on the results of this tool, then Part A has been successful. It is possible to take the examination in a variety of languages, which will assist in reaching large numbers of people in various regions of the world. The Adult ADHD Rating Scale (ASRS) is an important diagnostic tool because it assists in estimating the prevalence of ADHD, as well as the signs and symptoms associated with it, the risk factors associated with it, and the impact that ADHD has on the individual, the community, and the general population.

A minimum of four or more symptoms must be scored from section A for the test to be declared positive and likely for the diagnosis of ADHD. For a diagnosis to be made, a minimum of four or more symptoms must be scored.

The adult self-assessment scale includes a section called Section B, which is composed of twelve questions. These questions serve to provide more information and investigate further the symptoms that patients are experiencing in greater depth and clarity. Because component B is not used for diagnosis but to provide extra information, there is no score that is specified for it.

Chapter 3:

Can Adult ADHD Be Cured?

Wouldn't it be beautiful if people around the world perceived neurodevelopmental abnormalities such as attention deficit hyperactivity disorder, learning disabilities, and autism differently? What if, instead of focusing on the difficulties presented by these disparities, we all tried to recognize the opportunities that these differences present?

What Is Neurodiversity?

Approaching ADHD from a neurodiverse point of view comes with the idea that your symptoms are not issues that should be "cured," but just a result of how differently your brain operates. *Neurodiversity* is a valid identity, much like different racial and gender identities. The term revolves around the idea that certain forms of mental disorders are only due to natural differences in the human brain. Neurodiversity helps people understand that those with different behaviors tend to have certain positive traits too. Having a short attention span does not mean your whole life is doomed because you have other positive qualities that you can take advantage of.

An example that shows this is how some people living with ADHD may struggle to organize their time effectively but display a great deal of enthusiasm and energy when doing things. If it is in a workplace, you may realize the positivity they have can uplift other people around. Although someone with ADHD may arrive late at a family gathering, they can easily become the life of the party once they get there because they will come up with exciting ways to enjoy it. Back in professional settings, their lack of restraint can work in their favor because it allows them to speak up when other people would be too collected to do so.

ADHD is a neurodevelopmental condition, which means that its symptoms, as well as the behaviors and characteristics that are associated with it, are the result of one's brain developing in a unique way than the average person's. These growth differences take place during the key stages of fetal development or after birth. ADHD is not the same as mental illness, which describes patterns of behavior in which an individual perceives a distinct state of mind from their normal self.

Although some individuals who have neurodivergent traits may have to make certain sacrifices, such as staying near their workplaces or schools, most of them have the potential to think comprehensively and unconventionally.

When associating with someone who is neurodivergent, it is important to keep your language respectful and not make assumptions about how they might want to interact with you. You can directly ask them about their preferences and try to understand their decisions.

Here are more positive sides of the neurodivergence coin:

- Many people who are neurodivergent can recognize their areas of great strength.

  o Having a good understanding of one's own capabilities is a priceless asset. People living with ADHD and other neurodivergent conditions have spent a lot of time devising strategies that allow them to overcome their challenges and realize their full potential. Thinking differently allows them to figure out what their brain does and find appropriate settings to flourish. This is a valid advantage because it is quite challenging for people who have similar ways of thinking to identify their mental pillars.

- They can establish connections.

  o Individuals who have neurodivergent conditions can make connections others miss, and that is a significant benefit. Some of them can channel their focus on specific information and see links between things that may appear to have no bearing on one another. They can channel their focus toward understanding the bigger picture.

To embrace neurodiversity, inquire about others' conditions by asking them to describe their symptoms and situations. Strive to understand not only the areas in which people require assistance but also their areas of great strength. Always pay great attention to what they willingly share with you because disclosing personal information does not come easily to everyone. If someone who is neurodivergent shares information with you, it gives you a clear insight into why they need support and which areas require change.

When talking to someone who is neurodivergent, allow them time to reflect and react to your question. Refrain from interrupting or hurrying them through what they are saying because they may need enough time to process your discussion.

If you live with someone who is neurodivergent, try making fair adjustments by ensuring that the setting aligns with their capabilities and does not interfere with their wellness or the ability to concentrate. This is a valid measure because there are times when being in certain situations can hurt their emotions. You can also help your loved ones to interact as they wish by supplying them with sensory objects and communication tools.

Other Neurodivergent Conditions

ADHD has friends, it is not the only neurodevelopmental condition out there. Sometimes mental health providers confuse ADHD for its friends and vice versa, but in other cases, they occur together, like siblings from the same mother.

Autism

If you or your loved one have trouble concentrating on the tasks at hand, you may worry that they suffer from attention deficit hyperactivity disorder. Are you having trouble prioritizing your schedule? Do you find it challenging to finish one appointment before moving on to another exciting adventure? All of these are signs that you may have ADHD. These symptoms correspond to what most people know about the prevalent neurodevelopmental condition. If you go to see a medical professional, ADHD may be the first condition that surfaces in their mind. However, ADHD is not always the main cause of the problem, and sometimes it is not even the issue.

Individuals who have autism often show symptoms of ADHD, so they can be misdiagnosed with ADHD. Prior to determining whether a person has attention deficit hyperactivity disorder, clinicians apply their awareness of how the disorder might be confused with other conditions such as autism, as well as how the situation becomes when the two conditions overlap.

Autism spectrum disorder (ASD) refers to a range of illnesses that have an impact on behavior as well as on communication and development. The symptoms of ASD and ADHD may share a common cause, which is why it can be challenging to differentiate between the two conditions. Both conditions can take place at the same time. For instance, some individuals who have ADHD may exhibit symptoms that do not fall within the diagnostic criteria for ADHD. These symptoms may include strong focus and concentration on a single item.

Learning Disabilities

Learning disabilities are conditions that interfere with a person's capacity to perform mathematical calculations, comprehend or use spoken or written language, direct attention, or coordinate actions. Examples of learning disabilities include *dyslexia* and *dyscalculia*. The learning disability, called dyscalculia, involves serious challenges in mathematical problems. Dyslexia involves trouble recognizing speech sounds and learning the link between the sounds and the letters or words they represent. Learning disabilities and ADHD have similar impacts on individuals, such as working low-income jobs after failing to keep better positions at work.

ADHD is not a learning disability, but it may make it difficult to learn. Certain symptoms of ADHD, such as having trouble concentrating, can cause an individual to encounter certain difficulties in the educational process. However, living with ADHD should not prevent an individual from pursuing their academic goals and aspirations. People living with ADHD have the potential to become successful students, be it at the tertiary level or anywhere in life. Individuals who have ADHD have the potential to succeed even in environments that demand a high level of attentiveness and a calm environment if they receive the appropriate therapy and support.

Untreated Adult ADHD

If individuals with ADHD do not receive treatment for the disorder, the condition may have substantial consequences for their lives. Even their close friends or relatives who live in the same house may suffer the impact of the condition.

Adult ADHD may go untreated due to several reasons, such as lack of proper knowledge, fear of stigmatization, and not having a diagnosis. Regardless of what one's reasons are, if the condition remains untreated, it may connect to several risks, including the following:

- Conflict in interpersonal relationships.

- Mental health issues, such as low self-esteem, sadness, and anxiety.

- Job instability.

- Misuse of alcohol and other substances.

- Unfavorable interactions between parents and their children.

- A rise in the overall death rate due to safety concerns such as unseen distractions while driving.

ADHD is NOT curable, but it is also not something to be ashamed of. Do not lose heart and sulk because you are stronger than it is. Although you are neurodiverse in a neurotypical world, you can still thrive and find happiness through it all. It is not your fault if the systems in place are not tailored to your needs. All you need is the right guidance and support. Instead of looking at ADHD as a disability, why not embrace it as an identity?

Chapter 4:

What Conditions Are

Comorbid with Adult ADHD?

Comorbidity is the word used in medicine to describe the presence of two or more conditions existing at the same time. In general, people who are living with ADHD are more likely to have other behavior disorders, both of which can make it difficult for them to operate well in daily life. Between sixty percent and eighty percent of people who have ADHD also have another disorder. Let us go through the most common comorbid disorders that can coexist with ADHD (Katzman et al., 2017).

Depression

It is not uncommon for ADHD patients to also suffer from depression. It is possible to have both conditions at the same time, which is why medical professionals sometimes refer to them as comorbid or coexisting conditions.

ADHD is a condition that makes it difficult to focus on one thing, as explained earlier in other chapters. Those who are affected by it, whether they are children or adults, may have difficulty completing tasks, remaining still, or remembering things like appointments or specifics.

Depression is when one experiences overwhelming melancholy and despondency daily for a period of at least two weeks at a time. It may be difficult to carry out daily functions, such as going to school, working, or sleeping.

Statistics estimate that up to 30% of children diagnosed with ADHD also suffer from a serious mood disorder such as depression. In addition, there are professionals who believe that more than half of the individuals who have the condition will seek treatment for depression at some point in their lives.

Having ADHD increases one's risk of clinical depression by a factor of four. Those who are hyperactive and impulsive are also more likely to take their own lives, making this risk even more severe for them. Depression is a potential side effect of attention deficit hyperactivity disorder (ADHD), particularly if the condition goes untreated. This form of secondary depression develops as a direct result of the persistent frustration and disappointment that many people who have ADHD go through in their daily lives.

Because some of the signs and symptoms of ADHD and depression are like one another, it can be challenging to identify and treat either illness. For instance, having problems focusing is one of the symptoms of both depression and ADHD. In addition, if you use medication to treat the symptoms of ADHD, the medication may interfere with your ability to sleep or alter your eating patterns, both of which are part of the symptoms of depression. Both attention deficit hyperactivity disorder (ADHD) and major depressive disorder (MDD) can cause hyperactivity and irritability in young ones.

When people have a challenging time managing the symptoms of their ADHD, this can also lead to depression. It is possible that children will have trouble having a good relationship with their classmates or friends during play, while adults may have problems at work. This may result in profound emotions of hopelessness, as well as other symptoms of depression.

Depression can cause a range of psychological and physical symptoms. By now you already know the signs and symptoms of ADHD. So, let us look at the signs and symptoms of depression for comparison and differentiation shake.

Signs and symptoms of depression may include:

- Difficulty concentrating or making decisions.

- Unusually slow or agitated movements.

- Persistent depressed mood.

- Loss of interest or pleasure in hobbies and activities.

- Changes in appetite and body weight.

- Excessive feelings of guilt or worthlessness.

- Decreased energy or fatigue.

- Difficulty sleeping or oversleeping.

- Thoughts of death or suicide, or suicide attempts.

A doctor may determine that a patient has depression if they have five of these signs and symptoms throughout the course of the same two-week period. In addition to these symptoms, depression can also result in irritability, agitation, chronic pain, headaches, and gastrointestinal issues.

Some signs of ADHD symptoms in individuals suffering from depression may include:

- Trouble concentrating and staying focused.

- Impulsivity.

- Excessive attention to one activity.

- Emotional difficulties, including the inability to manage emotions such as anger or frustration.

- Extreme disorganization.

- Hyperactivity or restlessness.

- Disorganization and forgetfulness.

- Inattentiveness.

ADHD and Depression Treatment

People living with ADHD can experience side effects from the medication they take. One of these side effects can enhance pre-existing symptoms of depression or the drugs themselves can create symptoms that are like those of depression. This can also make it more challenging to diagnose depression in patients who simultaneously have ADHD.

Because of this, it may be difficult to distinguish between the two disorders and treat them in the appropriate manner. However, unlike depression, ADHD typically continues throughout a person's entire life.

Anyone who suspects that the medication they take for ADHD could be causing symptoms of depression should seek the opinion of a qualified medical professional. Medication and therapy may be recommended by a physician for people diagnosed with ADHD or ADHD in combination with depression.

Medication Treatment

Medication is an additional treatment option for mental health conditions such as depression and ADHD the other being therapy which we will look at soon. Both ADHD and depression have been related to low levels of the neurotransmitter dopamine in the brain. Dopamine is important for enjoyment, focus, and motivation, just to mention a few functions. The levels of dopamine in the brain are attempted to be raised by a number of antidepressants and ADHD drugs.

Stimulants are a type of drug that is widely used for ADHD. Stimulants work by increasing the amount of dopamine in the brain. These prescription drugs are offered in both immediate-release and extended-release formulations. Methylphenidate and amphetamine are two examples of stimulants that are commonly administered to treat attention deficit hyperactivity disorder (ADHD) (Concerta and Ritalin). Taking these drugs has been demonstrated to not only treat depression but also lower the likelihood of having it in the future.

Antidepressants are a class of medications that are prescribed to patients suffering from a variety of mental health disorders, including anxiety and depression. There are several types of antidepressants, the most prevalent of which are tricyclics, selective serotonin reuptake inhibitors (SSRIs), and serotonin-norepinephrine reuptake inhibitors. Tricyclics are the oldest type of antidepressant, dating back to the early 1900s (SNRIs). Sertraline and paroxetine are examples of SSRIs, which are the kind of antidepressants that are most frequently administered. A prescription of antidepressant drugs can help ease symptoms of both depression and ADHD.

Atypical antidepressants like bupropion work by altering the levels of the neurotransmitter's dopamine and norepinephrine in the brain. Although it is an antidepressant, there is evidence that it can also assist relieve some ADHD symptoms.

People or caregivers of people living with ADHD should monitor behavioral changes and look out for signs of depression or another behavioral or mood disorder and should inform their physician.

Therapy Treatment

Therapy is a common treatment for mental health conditions and is used in treating ADHD and depression. There is a wide variety of therapeutic modalities available for the treatment of depression. Both cognitive behavioral therapy (also known as CBT) and interpersonal therapy (also known as ITP) are examples of evidence-based methods of treatment that have been demonstrated to be successful in improving the outcome of ADHD and depression.

The primary goals of cognitive behavioral therapy (CBT) are to assist people in recognizing and altering problematic thought patterns, as well as learning new methods to deal with stress.

Interpersonal Therapy (TP) operates under the presumption that there is a significant correlation between emotional distress and difficulties in interpersonal relationships. As a result, its primary goal is to assist you in enhancing the quality of connections with others so that a person with ADHD with depression can experience a reduction in their symptoms.

The goal of treatment for attention deficit hyperactivity disorder is normally to teach you techniques that will help you improve your attention and focus, as well as your behavioral control. CBT is an effective treatment for both depression and ADHD, making it a useful therapeutic option for persons who suffer from both disorders at the same time. People who have ADHD can benefit from recognizing and modifying harmful patterns of thinking as well as acquiring skills that can help improve attention, organization, time management, behavioral control, and stress management. These skills can be found in a variety of educational settings.

If you also suffer from depression, you should look for a therapist that specializes in treating clients who have both ADHD and depression. When looking for a therapist, do not be afraid to inquire about their previous patients' experiences with ADHD and depression, as well as the method of treatment that they employ for patients suffering from these diseases.

Anxiety

This refers to the mental and physiological reaction that we have in response to something that we perceive to be dangerous or threatening. The fight-or-flight response, which entails either remaining to fight or running away from danger, is more commonly connected with fear, which is an emotional reaction to an imminent threat... Fear can be caused by either an external or internal threat.

People who suffer from anxiety disorders may find themselves trying to avoid situations that bring on or exacerbate their symptoms. Performance at work, in school, and in personal relationships can all be negatively impacted. Anxiety disorders include but are not limited to social anxiety disorder, panic attacks, PTSD, and others.

In general, a person's anxiety must meet both of the following criteria to be diagnosed with an anxiety disorder:

- Be out of proportion to the situation or age inappropriate.

- Hinder the ability to function normally.

Both anxiety and ADHD are closely related conditions. The most common comorbidities associated with ADHD are anxiety disorders. This is due, in no small part, to the fact that living with ADHD results in a life that is marked by stress and worry.

The diagnostic criteria for ADHD do not specifically include anxiety as a separate condition; however, there is a strong correlation between the two conditions. People who are living with attention deficit hyperactivity disorder (ADHD) are twice as likely to have an anxiety disorder as those who do not suffer from the condition, whose percentages are close to 50%.

Symptoms of anxiety disorders vary depending on the type of anxiety disorder you have. Some common symptoms of an anxiety disorder include:

- mental symptoms:

  o Intense, uncontrollable thoughts.

- Recurring memories or flashbacks of catastrophic events.

- Experiencing fear, panic, and unease.

- Nightmares.

- physical symptoms:

  - Heart palpitations.

  - Numbness or tingling in hands or feet.

  - Shortness of breath.

  - Cold or sweaty hands.

  - Nausea.

  - Dry mouth.

  - Muscle tension.

- behavioral symptoms:

  - Ritualistic actions, such as continuously washing hands.

  - Inability to remain quiet and steady.

  - Difficulty sleeping.

Does ADHD Make Anxiety Worse?

Researchers found that issues related to individuals with ADHD, such as tardiness, procrastination, and the possibility of social stigma, all caused participants to suffer anxiety at various periods in their life.

People who have been diagnosed with both ADHD and an anxiety illness typically present with increased levels of anxiety than individuals who do not have ADHD. However, although they may not fulfill the diagnostic criteria for anxiety, people with ADHD may still occasionally and in certain situations experience it during their regular lives. This is specifically due to the ADHD, which may cause time blindness, poor working memory, and exaggerated emotions, among other symptoms that produce anxiety.

Treatment of ADHD and Anxiety

It may be difficult to treat both attention deficit hyperactivity disorder and anxiety at the same time since certain ADHD drugs might make anxiety symptoms worse. However, treatment is necessary for both disorders. It is possible that your doctor will prioritize treating the ailment that is having the most impact on your overall quality of life. They might also offer advice on how to deal with the other ailment they have diagnosed.

The following are some of the treatments that your physician may suggest for both ADHD and anxiety:

- prescription medication
- cognitive and behavioral therapy
- meditation
- relaxation techniques

It is essential to communicate honestly and openly with your medical provider regarding your symptoms. This is especially important to keep in mind if you have reason to believe that you are coping with more than one condition at the same time. Your doctor will want to know if a treatment is making either of your diseases worse, so be sure to tell him or her if this is the case. That information will assist them in customizing your treatment.

Other Coping Mechanisms for ADHD and Anxiety Today

- Continue taking the medicine prescribed for ADHD, and if necessary, do not feel lazy to go to your psychotherapy sessions as well. Continue taking the medication prescribed for ADHD, and if necessary, keep going to your psychotherapy sessions as well. Medication can help reduce the symptoms of ADHD, as well as improve coping and functioning, making it easier for adults with ADHD to feel more in control of their lives and overall reducing their anxiety levels. The same can be said for psychotherapy, which can now be done remotely in widespread availability.

- Maintain healthy habits. Keep up with your healthy routines. Many people, regardless of whether they have ADHD with anxiety or not, are reporting feelings of general overload and chronic stress for which they cannot identify a specific cause. Effective ways to reduce overall stress include improving one's exercise routine, sleeping habits, and diet, as well as avoiding exposure to physical anxiety triggers such as caffeine and alcohol.

- Lower the bar on expectations. Reduce the level of excellence required. It is better to expect to be good enough than to expect to be flawless, and adopting this perspective is one of the first steps toward breaking free of a rut and experiencing less anxiety.

- Structure unstructured time. There is no getting around the fact that developing a routine is essential, particularly one that is obvious. Planners can be thought of as time managers because this enables us to see the future that is hours or days ahead, thereby preparing us for the activities that we have planned.

- Move around and get some exercise. Moving around is beneficial, as obvious as that may sound. You can walk around after work or jog a few blocks and back to ease your anxiety. This is especially important to keep in mind when confined to a small space and working from home. Movement in and of itself can serve as a type of meditation, providing a means by which you can detach yourself from the demands of your daily lives, be at work or at home.

- Get your actual spaces in order. Define the areas of the home that will be used for working, relaxing, sleeping, studying, and other activities to facilitate the behavioral priming and habit formation processes. Resetting and organizing your spaces so that they are ready for the next day can help reduce anxiety and ease the transition from one state to another.

- Specify tasks. Avoid activities with a hazy definition and instead pack your calendar with items that are centered on tasks or times. A task may be easily completed even when you do not want to do it by clearly outlining it in advance. This helps prevent front-end perfectionism. Soon after engagement, discomfort disappears.

Substance Use Disorder

Individuals who have ADHD have a significantly increased likelihood of acquiring substance use disorders. When compared to the general population, adolescents who have problems with substance use are more likely to also have attention deficit hyperactivity disorder. According to the findings of another study, 23% of young adults who have problems with substance use also have the syndrome.

Why Do Adults with ADHD Develop SUD?

Although experts are unsure of the precise causes of the association, they have various theories that link substance abuse to ADHD, including:

- The characteristics of ADHD, such as impulsivity, poor judgment, and the ensuing difficulties in education, may make someone more likely to start using drugs.

- People with ADHD may be tempted to use recreational medications to address their own symptoms.

- ADHD and the likelihood of developing a substance use disorder may be genetically linked.

Additionally, those who have ADHD and substance use disorders may have anatomical differences in their brains, such as a reduced size in the frontal cortex and the cerebellum. Cigarette smoking has an effect on the chance of developing substance use problems in adolescents and adults who have ADHD. For instance, a number of studies have shown that more than fifty percent of teenagers who smoke and both have attention deficit hyperactivity disorder (ADHD) go on to acquire substance use disorder as young adults. According to the findings of the study, this may be because friends who smoke may also use other substances. In addition, it was observed that nicotine use alters the structure of the developing brain.

Children who begin treatment for ADHD at an earlier age are at a lower risk of developing substance use disorders than their counterparts who begin therapy at a later age. In addition, it is crucial to treat mental health conditions, such as anxiety and depression, that frequently occur alongside ADHD. Doing so could lessen an individual's risk of getting into this danger. Anxiety and depression are two examples.

However, there is a complex relationship between ADHD and substance abuse, and additional research would be helpful in fully explaining this association.

Characteristics of ADHD that may contribute to addiction include:

- Feelings of guilt, fear, or disdain.
- Impulsiveness
- Uncontrolled anxiety.
- Reward seeking.

These characteristics, however, do not address the root causes of addiction, so we also must investigate risk factors of addition. The following are some common addiction risk factors:

- Difficulties with academic or professional performance.
- History of sexual abuse as a child.
- Mental health problems.
- Family members who have used drugs or support drug use.
- Past family conflict as a child.
- Friends who abuse drugs or encourage drug use.

Are Stimulant Drugs for ADHD Addictive?

Caregivers or people living with ADHD can worry that the stimulant medications (like Adderall) that they are prescribed to manage ADHD can be addictive. Stimulant drugs work by increasing levels of a neurotransmitter in the brain called dopamine, which helps increase focus and attention. Focus and attention are skills that people with ADHD frequently struggle to master.

Dopamine is a neurotransmitter that has been shown to influence mood as well as the experience of pleasure. This euphoria that it produces makes individuals want more. Concerns have been raised regarding the potential for addiction in people on ADHD stimulants because cocaine and other illegal substances also enhance dopamine levels.

People with ADHD have been seen taking stimulants that were not prescribed to them, according to some reports. Tablets of Ritalin have been broken up and inhaled, and the medication has also been mixed in water and administered intravenously. According to a number of studies, misusing Ritalin might result in dependence on the medication. On the other hand, the likelihood of Ritalin becoming addictive in either children or adults is significantly reduced when the medication is taken as directed.

Ritalin can produce effects that are comparable to those of cocaine when it is taken in quantities that are significantly higher than those that are normally given for ADHD. However, researchers have discovered significant distinctions between the two medications. The rate at which a drug increases dopamine levels in the body is one of the elements that might contribute to abuse and addiction to drugs. The risk of abuse increases in proportion to the rate at which dopamine levels rise. According to the findings, it takes about an hour for Ritalin to elevate dopamine levels in the brain, in contrast to the mere seconds required by ingested cocaine. Because the doses of Ritalin and other stimulants used to treat ADHD tend to be smaller and the effects of the drugs tend to last longer, there is less of a chance of becoming addicted to them. If you use any stimulant for an extended period, you run the risk of developing a phenomenon known as tolerance. Tolerance manifests itself when higher dosages of a controlled substance are required to produce the same effect. When this occurs, a medical professional may subsequently be more willing to consider treating ADHD with medications that do not contain stimulants.

So, can stimulants cause substance abuse?

The use of stimulants in the management of ADHD has caused concern on the possibility of experimenting with other kinds of drugs. It has been the purpose of a number of investigations to assess the possibility of a connection between stimulant medicine for ADHD that is administered and issues with substance misuse, and the findings of these investigations suggest that there is not a substantial connection.

One of the studies that lasted the longest and followed a group of one hundred boys diagnosed with ADHD for a period of ten years found that those boys who took stimulant drugs did not have an increased risk of substance usage in comparison to those boys who did not take the drugs. An earlier study by the same authors even suggested that the use of stimulants might help prevent later drug abuse and alcoholism in children with ADHD. This was hypothesized based on the fact that the symptoms of ADHD, which often lead to substance abuse problems, are relieved using stimulants. The sooner stimulants are introduced into the system, the less likely it is that the individual would develop an addiction to them later.

Treatment for ADHD with Substance Use Disorder

There is a wide variety of therapy options available for those struggling with addiction to substances. To determine the most effective course of treatment for the individual, a trained medical practitioner should conduct an evaluation. They ought to consider the specific circumstances of the individual as well as any concomitant problems with the individual's physical health, mental health, or social life. A combination of therapy and medicine is often what medical professionals advise their patients to do.

Medication has the potential to assist in the management of cravings, the alleviation of withdrawal symptoms, and the prevention of relapse. Additionally, therapy can assist individuals in better comprehending the reasons behind their substance abuse, boosting their self-esteem, teaching them good coping techniques, and addressing a variety of other mental health concerns.

The road to recovery is different for everyone, depending on the person and the circumstances, but it could include things like the following:

- substance-free communities
- cleansing the body of toxic substance

- psychotherapy
- support groups
- intensive outpatient programs
- medication management
- rehabilitation

Addiction and ADHD Medication

When you take ADHD medicine in therapeutic doses that a licensed medical practitioner prescribed, you reduce the likelihood of developing an addiction.

People who have Attention Deficit Hyperactivity Disorder (ADHD) may receive drug recommendations from their doctors, such as methylphenidate (Ritalin) or dextroamphetamine (Adderall). People who take stimulant drugs are better able to concentrate and keep their feelings under control. If people use them while following the supervision of a doctor, there is no reason to believe that they will lead to addiction or the improper use of substances. However, if they use them for non-medical reasons, such as trying to remain awake to study or work, they put themselves at danger of developing an addiction or abusing the substance.

In addition, there is no evidence to suggest that individuals who use stimulant drugs for ADHD are at an increased risk of developing a substance use disorder at a later point in their lives. Therefore, even though children who have ADHD have a higher risk of substance use disorders, this is due to the condition itself and not the stimulant medicine that they take.

Reaching Out for Help

People who misuse substances have the best chance of preventing themselves from developing an addiction or a drug use disorder if they seek help as soon as they recognize their problem and before the condition worsens.

If a person has trouble keeping their substance usage under control, they should discuss the issue with their primary care physician. A physician can make treatment recommendations or send a patient to an appropriate specialist for care. It is now possible for professionals to successfully treat substance use disorders with minimal recurrence rates. Recovery is also attainable for patients who receive therapy that is both all-encompassing and ongoing.

Having ADHD can make day-to-day life difficult for a person, but there are ways that can make life easier for someone who has ADHD. People who are having trouble controlling the symptoms of ADHD or who would benefit from speaking with others who are going through the same thing can get support from others who are in the same boat.

People who are interested in learning more about the help and information that are available for individuals with ADHD can join a local or online group to discover more. Increasing people's awareness of

ADHD is also very crucial to our overall comprehension of the disorder.

Chapter 5:

What Coping Mechanisms

Can I Use to Manage

Symptoms of Adult ADHD?

Did you know? Medication is not the only way of solving your ADHD puzzle.

There should not be any version of your life where ADHD makes a complete mess of your life when you know you have it. Receiving a diagnosis helps you realize why you have certain challenges in specific areas of your life, and that is how you cope. When planning to regain control over your life, you first need to identify the elements that make it difficult for you to reign. What is your weakness? Impulsivity? Poor time management? Disorganization?

After you figure that part out, you can then devise strategies to deal with the weaknesses or create situations where your weaknesses are strengths. If you feel your weakness cannot be a strength, you can find ways to manage it before it cripples your mind! In this chapter, you will learn about how you can use some coping mechanisms to manage ADHD.

Creating To-Do Lists

Using to-do lists can help you or your loved one avoid running late or missing deadlines. People who struggle with ADHD may have trouble completing assignments and other projects, attending meetings on time, or completing chores and running errands. With a well-planned list of what you are supposed to do and when you should do it, you can rest well, knowing you can stay on top of your schedule. Your list of things to accomplish does not have to be a traditional pen and paper list format, but if you prefer to do things the old school way, then grab that paper and jot it away if you are prone to boredom and prefer to take advantage of the modern-day technology. You can use visual components such as stickers to make your lists look more creative. For convenience, you can create and store the lists on your phone or computer, but if that does not work for you, then try printing the lists out and sticking them in strategic positions. If your to-do list is for work-related responsibilities, you can stick it near your desk. If it is about what you should cook and when to drop your laundry, you can stick the list in your kitchen.

You should also try dividing your to-do lists into four quadrants based on the importance and urgency of each task. Separate the important tasks from the less important ones then determine which of the important tasks are also urgent. Separate the urgent work from tasks that can wait, then prioritize the important and urgent tasks.

This scheduling system helps you avoid feeling overwhelmed when you are close to deadlines or when the day is about to end but you still have dozens of things to do. In addition to that, using to-do lists addresses time myopia, a prevalent challenge among those who are living with ADHD. If you find that the average to-do list does not work for you, switch the game up and devise a system that is tailored to your individual way of living.

Journaling

Because of our difficulty paying attention, people who have ADHD frequently struggle with distracting and racing thoughts. You could find that keeping a journal helps you make sense of your ideas and eliminates the need for distractions. Put on paper whatever dominates the most real estate in your thoughts. You are not required to do it on a regular basis; you are free to keep a journal whenever you feel the need to clear some space in your thoughts.

Writing in a journal can help you process your feelings, particularly when you are feeling overwhelmed or frustrated. This exercise can help you untangle your thoughts and make sense of what you are feeling, even when they are racing around in your head too quickly or when you are suffering brain fog . Writing in a journal can assist those with ADHD or other neurological differences manage their irritation and reduce the frequency and intensity of angry outbursts.

Meditating

Practicing meditation teaches the mind to keep its attention fixed on a single idea. When you are feeling overwhelmed, it is also helpful in calming you down. People who have ADHD may find it challenging to meditate, particularly when they are trying it for the first time; therefore, it is recommended that they begin with breathing exercises and yoga.

Exercise your breathing by taking a deep breath for seven seconds, holding it for four, and then releasing it slowly for seven seconds. Count on each inhalation and exhalation to help you silence distracting mental chatter and concentrate solely on the physical activity at hand.

Practicing yoga combines mental reflection with physical movement. It is also beneficial for bringing both inattentiveness and hyperactivity under control.

Watching Your Budget

Sometimes, people with ADHD may splurge on items they do not really need. Although other individuals who do not have the condition may also be guilty of unnecessary spending, it tends to hit differently when one has a condition that interferes with their cognition. Budgeting money requires planning, time, and effort. If people with ADHD fail to keep their budgets in check, they may risk drowning in debt, going back and forth on important plans, neglecting bills, or even worsening their situations due to the stress that comes from a lack of resources.

If you or your partner has just been diagnosed with ADHD, you may want to learn how to manage your finances, so you save yourself from the hustle of having to do it after the time passes. If one does not have enough self-control to hold back whenever they want to spend excessively, it is a good practice to ditch credit cards and avoid getting loans. Living within one's means helps avoid the stress and anxiety of repaying debts.

Exercising

One short walk a day keeps the psychiatrist away. Is that right?

Exercise lessens the severity of ADHD symptoms and improves executive functions. Sometimes, when you are having trouble getting your work done because you cannot focus, all you need is a walk in the park. You will learn more about exercise and ADHD as you read further in this book, but you are also welcomed to carry out your own research.

Keeping Track of Your Strengths

We all must deal with difficult situations and fight against our problems. You will not be able to make progress if you keep dwelling on your past mistakes, so try to forgive yourself and go on. Create a list of the areas in which you are successful, the things you are good at, and those you do not require you to invest too much energy in. Take your time thinking about the qualities that light up your world, then put your attention on the things you are already good at, and work on improving those skills even further.

Playing Brain Games

Using brain games as a treatment alternative for ADHD improves *neuroplasticity*. The term refers to the capacity of one's brain to change and adapt as a response to new information and experiences. It is also called neural or brain plasticity.

Neuroplasticity has a number of advantageous effects for one's brain. The brain's ability to adapt can help promote:

- its capacity to acquire new knowledge and skills.

- one's capacity to improve upon their already established cognitive talents.

- a quicker recovery following neurological difficulties such as strokes and head trauma.

- improved functionality in areas where it became weak.

- improvements for brain wellness.

Brain-training games are played by people of all ages with the goals of enhancing mental functioning and delaying the aging process in the brain. Playing these games and participating in these activities, which are likely to increase your mental focus and fitness, is a great way to exercise your brain while also having an enjoyable time. Adults who have attention deficit hyperactivity disorder might improve their cognitive abilities by spending some of their time playing brain games like crossword puzzles and sudoku.

Outsourcing

Acknowledging your strengths does not rid you of weaknesses, so you should also remember the areas where you fall short. Realize there are other people who excel at what you need to improve, and others who need help with what you are good at. Find people who are exceptional in the areas that give you endless headaches and become a team. If your main problem is finishing projects, for example, you might want to consider forming a partnership with an individual who is skilled at bringing things to a successful conclusion. At work, you can also work together with one of your coworkers who excels in mathematics if you have a knack for design but struggle with numbers. Outsourcing helps fill gaps by providing solutions to the challenges that the ADHD symptoms present in the important areas of your life that are important to you.

Sleeping

Sleep deprivation can exacerbate the symptoms of adult ADHD, making it more difficult to deal with stressful situations and keep your attention on the task at hand during the day. Many adults who have ADHD have trouble falling asleep or staying in dreamland throughout the night. However, if you are going to try increasing your attention span, you will need to give your mind and body a break. The first thing you must do to get better rest is to determine how much sleep you need. To feel rejuvenated, some individuals require seven hours of sleep, but others let their dreams unfold for about eight to nine. After that, check to establish that you do not have any sleep disorders. If you are having trouble falling asleep, you can try taking melatonin or using another sleep aid.

Before you resort to sleeping tablets, however, ensure that your lack of sleep is due to other factors besides eating, consuming alcohol, or using electronics during bedtime. Some adults use caffeine to help them fall asleep, but others find that even decaffeinated tea keeps them too active. Should you want to try the hack, you will have to work on getting the timing right because if you take it too late, you might be too wired past the time you wanted to sleep and if you take it too early, you are most likely to miss your long-awaited ticket to the land of dreams. Watching your activities during the day can also have a significant impact on the quality of sleep you experience at night.

Chapter 6:

What Non-Pharmaceutical

Treatment Options Are

Available for Adult ADHD?

With ADHD, everyone has their battle, but the result depends on how one fights. Even though ADHD is not curable, there are strategies to make symptoms more manageable. Changing your attitude toward your condition can help with symptom management. An adult woman called Anna struggled with symptoms of ADHD and watched it almost ruin her life, but she gradually realized she could take charge of her situation by making some changes to her lifestyle. She produced strategies to manage her situation, and with time, Anna could focus and carry out demanding tasks better than before.

Adults with attention deficit hyperactivity disorders have difficulties in managing their symptoms and do not want to take ADHD medication due to the side effects the medication has. Non-drug treatment options have been established, which are as effective as the medication. ADHD talk therapy, which involves talking to a therapist to help with implementing strategies to better manage life, the type of therapy to choose is an individual decision. The following are the different non-drug methods which can be used to treat adult ADHD.

Behavior Management Interventions

Behavior management interventions are often used in children, especially those in school age. A specialist will equip the parents with proper parenting skills to help their children manage ADHD symptoms. Even though these interventions are mostly used in children, adults can also use them to manage their own symptoms, tailoring these strategies to fit their current responsibilities.

There are distinct categories of behavioral interventions which treat adult ADHD. Examples include:

- cognitive-behavioral interventions
- contingency management

Behavioral therapy techniques use reinforcement, punishment, shaping, modeling, and related techniques to change behavior. These techniques have the benefit of being highly focused, which produce fast and effective results.

Cognitive modification focuses on identifying and changing thinking errors or inaccurate thinking.

Behavioral modification makes the environment more conducive to concentration and focus. It involves learning what strengthens and maintains problem behaviors and creates systems that favor constructive behaviors and support an individual's ability to function well. Cognitive behavioral therapy (CBT) is the most common and effective non-pharmaceutical treatment option for ADHD. This type of counseling teaches individuals specific skills to manage the behavior and change negative thinking patterns into positive outcomes in behavior, self-control, and self-esteem. Treatment occurs one on one, in couples or groups. However, one on one formants are mostly used to improve focus, productivity, and time management. Mostly, treatment begins with psychoeducation, during which an individual learns about the disorder and reasons for their treatment. Psychoeducation is followed by an organization module which helps the acquisition of different techniques, such as:

- goal setting
- sequencing and prioritizing
- planning time schedules
- using calendars
- making to do lists
- monitoring progress
- planning breaks

Individuals also learn problem-solving strategies for articulating problems more clearly, creating a list of solutions, evaluating them, and testing the chosen solutions. A distraction treatment module enables an individual to recognize their attention span and arrange tasks according to that. It introduces skills for dealing with the distractions, such as writing them down and going back to the task using alarms.

Usually, a therapist meets a client once or twice in a week. Cognitive behavioral therapy sessions identify situations where planning, organization, time, and task management are a problem in an individual day-to-day life. It helps individuals deal with obligations such as completing work on time, paying bills and it also provides personal fulfillment and well-being such as exercise, sleep. We will soon discuss more about CBT, but first, we must cover other elements of behavior management.

Contingency Management

Contingency management is another form of behavioral treatment intervention that involves a more intensive program of behavior change. The strategies used are to encourage specific behavior using rewards and consequences earned by the individual. These are amazingly effective in producing behavior modifications since the rules are spelled out clearly, preventing both parties (therapist and patient) from backing down on their promises.

Contingent Positive Consequences

Contingency positive consequences - I finished all my tasks today, so I'm rewarding myself with a nice dinner.

This strategy focuses on providing the individuals with positive consequences for behaving in appropriate ways. The system uses praise, rewards, and points to encourage appropriate behavior. The simple logic behind it is one can increase the frequency of a desired behavior by providing rewards when such behavior occurs. In adults, spouses and employers think about the kinds of behavior they want to encourage, like time management making sure the individual understands what you want him or her to do and then praising the individual, when observed to be occurring. When spouses or employers notice and appreciate their efforts, it frequently increases the desire to do so. Behavioral treatment also involves self-concrete which are tangible rewards for appropriate behavior. If the individual meets his/her obligations like a project at work, they can reward themselves with a nice dinner. Some of the rules for an effective use of positive reinforcement include:

- A *reinforcer* follows the behavior and is contingent on what is taking place of that behavior, that is, the behavior must take place before the reinforcer is given.

- A *consequence* comes in only when a reinforcer increases the occurrence of the behavior it follows. If the behavior does not change, the consequence is not serving as a reinforcer.

- Positive reinforcers can be socially such as praises, material in form of money or it can be an activity such as going for lunch.

To be most effective, reinforcement should always take place immediately after the behavior.

Contingent Negative Consequences

I will not let myself rest this weekend until I have cleaned my apartment.

Beside using positive reinforcement to encourage good behavior, behavioral treatment also depends on negative consequences or punishment to reduce undesirable behavior. This system uses time outs and response costs, such as losing points or rewards, to discourage inappropriate behavior. When a particular behavior is consistently followed by negative consequences, it diminishes in frequency and intensity. An example of a contingent negative is if the individual is not meeting obligations like not finishing work projects on time, the employer can punish them by cutting down on their salary. This will make the individual understand that there is no pay for bad behavior. Which will encourage the individual to now start working hard.

Effective Instruction Conveyance

I am not sure if I'm doing this task right, so I will ask my boss to give me clear and specific instructions.

This system is clear and specific. It provides room for individuals to openly ask where they do not understand.

When-Then Contingency Systems

When the semester is done, then I will start binge-watching this new TV show that I have been looking forward to seeing.

The when-then model of behavior is a method for comprehending and explaining human behavior. The context in which a behavior happens is given precedence in this model above the characteristics of people who engage in the conduct. This is done rather than focusing on the people who engage in the behavior.

Benefits of Behavior Management Interventions

- Increased self-esteem

    o Behavioral treatment interventions allow patients to build their self-esteem by focussing on problems and working towards a solution. As they find answers, their confidence grows and can conquer the disorder.

- Reinforced positive thoughts

    o ADHD patients have negative thought patterns that control their lives. Negative thinking becomes automatic with many individuals; cognitive behavioral therapy teaches patients how to turn negative thoughts into positive thoughts.

- Increased ability to plan and schedule activities

  - Behavioral therapy can help ADHD individuals to consistently plan activities, be responsible, organize daily schedules and manage time productively, making them meet their obligations and improve quality of life.

Other non-pharmaceutical treatment options for adult ADHD include *neurofeedback* and emotional therapy. Neurofeedback controls an individual's brain waves to increase brain function and boost their mental well-being.

Physiological Treatments

When dealing with ADHD, adults have the option to try physiological treatments before getting to drugs. These treatment strategies involve lifestyle changes such as regular exercises and dietary modifications to work around the symptoms of ADHD.

Physical Exercise

Exercise is a therapy option for ADHD that does not involve a physician's prescription or a visit to the office of a therapist. According to recent findings from research, engaging in regular physical activity can improve one's thinking abilities, and it may also reduce the symptoms of ADHD. Even just one session of physical activity can improve your motivation for mental work, raise your brainpower, give you energy, and help you feel less confused. Physical activity has a significant number of similar benefits for your brain as the ADHD drug you take.

However, to get these benefits, you will need to get the exercises right and work out for the appropriate time.

When choosing the ideal activity to deal with the symptoms of ADHD, pick one that

- is fun.

- needs you to stay alert.

- gets your heart racing.

- involves cooperation and interaction with others.

- connects with your inner being.

- requires you to make quick changes.

The trick is to look for a pastime that is compatible with your way of life and then to persist with it.

Cardio Exercises

This category involves activities that cause your heart to race. Your brain will develop new pathways because of cardio exercises, and it will also flood with hormones that make it easier to pay attention. You should engage in an activity that not only speeds up your heart rate but also holds it at that elevated level for a predetermined period, such as 25 to 30 minutes.

When trying cardio for management of ADHD symptoms, you start with one of these:

- walking fast
- swimming laps
- running
- biking

You are free to carry out these activities either outside or inside, but if you have the option, it is best to do them outside so nature can do its wonders too! According to several studies, reducing the severity of ADHD symptoms while moving outside in natural settings can be even more effective than exercising indoors.

Martial arts

The complexity of the activity you do determines how beneficial it is to your brain, so activities such as karate and judo place an emphasis on developing self-control while bringing your mind and body closer together.

When you practice martial arts, you gain skills such as:

- memory
- balance
- focus and concentration
- timing

Martial arts also refine your motor skills and help you

remember that actions have consequences. However, it is not an option for everyone. If martial arts are not your thing, some additional physical hobbies that will challenge both your body and your mind, you can find others:

Other daring physical activities include:

- dance
- yoga
- mountain climbing
- gymnastics

Team Sports

It is possible that taking part in a league of softball or soccer will be the impetus you need to get up and move about several times per week. The advantages of regular physical activity increase when you participate in organized sports because you have a social network to help keep you motivated.

Strength Training

If you are just getting started with an exercise routine, try to focus on aerobic exercises like walking or running to begin with. After you have been at it for a while, you can then mix things up by doing some weight training for a change of pace. Try out some exercises such as:

- pushups

- weightlifting
- squats
- lunges
- pullups

Weekly Exercise Routine

Many people who have ADHD tend to set their fitness objectives too high, putting themselves in almost impossible positions. Exaggerated goals decimate your chances to achieve them, and if you were to make the impossible possible, you would have to strain yourself. To begin, you need to determine the very least amount of physical activity that you will tolerate, such as exercising for thirty minutes twice per week. The next step is to determine an achievable maximum exercise target, such as working out for half an hour twice each week. There is a strong probability that you will not have trouble accomplishing your minimum exercise targets, and there is also a good chance that you will go above and beyond your maximum target. When you achieve your goals, it gives you a sense of satisfaction that pushes you to continue your training routine. Keep in mind that both your minimum and maximum targets should increase with time.

When training yourself to establish a stable workout routine, you should:

- Hold yourself accountable.

If you promised yourself that you would work out

before the end of the day, you should not back out of that commitment. Should you get too busy to exercise outside or go to the gym, try doing some push-ups, or running around instead. Your aim for the day should be to do what you promised yourself you would.

- Keep track of your workouts.

You can try to maintain a record of your weekly exercises by putting up a calendar and cross off the days on which you completed your workouts. Marking the days that you have to workout will help you create a routine and stay on track. Remember to keep the planning simple; there is no need for you to make commitments for an entire year if you will not even manage to stick to it for a few months. You can start by setting the workout goals you want to achieve within four weeks, then strive to follow through.

- Do not sabotage your efforts.

Many adults who are living with ADHD have an inner voice that lurks in the back of their minds, waiting for any chance to sabotage them.

If you hear a voice inside your head suggesting that you skip your workout for the day and do it the next day instead, tell it to get lost! Giving in to a lazy inner voice will make it difficult for you to establish consistent physical activity routines.

Diet

What you eat every day has an impact on how you live as a person. People who eat right have fewer chances of suffering from most health problems. Those who make poor diet choices run the risk of worsening their symptoms or even draining the strength of their medications. When you cook meals for yourself or someone living with ADHD, make sure to keep them simple but nutritious.

Why is Diet Important for Adults with ADHD?

Children and adults with attention deficit hyperactivity disorder (ADHD) may experience a worsening of their symptoms if they do not consume enough of specific types of foods. The good news is that a diet designed for ADHD that includes proper amounts of the right nutrients can improve brain function and reduce the severity of symptoms to an extent.

Anna realized her behavior is easier to manage when she consumes a diet that is nutritious and contains enough vegetables, fruits, and complex carbohydrates in addition to enough protein. Some may think it is too costly, but promoting better health is always worth it. Besides, you can devise other cost-friendly methods such as cultivating a small garden in your backyard so you do not have to buy every onion and tomato you eat, for instance.

Protein for ADHD Brain Function

There is some evidence that eating foods that are rich in protein, such as lean beef, pig, chicken, fish, eggs, beans, nuts, soy, and low-fat dairy products, can have a positive impact on the symptoms of ADHD. Consuming foods that have a high protein content enables your body to produce *neurotransmitters*, which are the chemicals your brain cells secrete to connect with one another. Eating protein also prevents blood sugar spikes, which are linked to increased hyperactivity and impulsivity.

Strive to eat a meal that contains protein in the morning so that your body can produce the brain-away neurotransmitters that it needs to be a little daring and go an extra mile by looking there. Additionally, you can find opportunities to sneak in some lean protein at various times during the day. These can be nutritious snack bars or even a high protein salad.

Vitamins and Minerals

According to certain research findings ADHD is associated with deficiencies in several micronutrients, including iron, magnesium, zinc, vitamin B-6, and vitamin D. These are all required elements in the diet and consuming foods that contain them is not likely to result in any negative consequences.

People can find these nutrients in the following foods:

- vitamin D

- o mushrooms, fatty fish, soy milk, and fortified cereal

- iron: beef liver, leafy vegetables, and beans

- magnesium: almonds, pumpkin seeds, spinach, and peanuts

- zinc: shellfish, avocados, beans, grass-fed lamb, and broccoli

- vitamin B-6: chickpeas, eggs, bananas, potatoes, and prunes

More Complex Carbohydrates.

Carbs are the masters of the game and should be the life of your diet if you are living with ADHD. Eating foods that contain complex carbohydrates makes you feel satisfied for a longer period, which then discourages you from aimlessly nibbling on other food items that are high in sugar. These carbs also have the potential to improve your quality of sleep if you consume them in the hours leading up to your bedtime. Be sure to drop a lot of veggies and various fruits onto your plate. Stock fruits such as oranges, apples, kiwis, grapefruit, and pears, among other options. If you eat this kind of meal in the evening, it can make it easier for you to go to sleep.

The foods below contain complex carbohydrates:

- beans and lentils

- vegetables

- fruits

- brown rice

- whole-grain bread and past

More Omega-3 Fatty Acids

One's diet is the only source through which they can obtain the vital omega-3 fatty acids. They have a positive impact on both the cardiovascular system and the nervous system. Tuna, salmon, and other white fish that live in cold waters are some good sources of omega-3 fatty acids. There are a variety of different foods, such as walnuts, canola oil, Brazil nuts, flaxseeds, and olive oil, that also have omega-3 fatty acids. An individual may also consider taking a supplement that contains omega-3 fatty acids. To aid in the treatment of ADHD, the Food and Drug Administration granted approval for the omega compound known as Vayarin.

It is possible that people with ADHD may have lower levels of omega-3 fats in their bodies. According to the findings of certain studies, increasing one's intake of omega-3 fatty acids may contribute to a slight improvement in symptoms. That also means that taking omega-3 fatty acids may help those living with ADHD increase their focus, memory, motivation, and attention to demanding activities. However, it is important to conduct additional study and not regard omega-3 fatty acids as a suitable replacement for ADHD medication.

Nutritional Supplements for ADHD

Some medical professionals suggest that individuals

who have ADHD take supplements that have vitamins and minerals daily. However, other nutrition authorities say that those who consume a balanced diet that do not require additional micronutrient intake.

Note that taking multivitamins is safe for people who do not get enough nutrients in their diet but having excessive amounts of vitamins can be harmful. Because the signs and symptoms of ADHD tend to differ from person to person, individuals with ADHD should discuss supplements with their primary care physicians before incorporating them into their diets.

Foods to Limit or Avoid

Some foods seem to worsen symptoms of ADHD, so people with it may feel better if they consume with caution. If you or your loved one has ADHD, they should try to limit or avoid the following:

Sugar

Consuming foods high in sugar can cause blood glucose levels to jump and then crash, which can have an impact on one's energy levels. Some parents and caregivers of children with ADHD have seen a correlation between the amount of sugar their charges consume and their level of hyperactivity.

Although some study points to a correlation between consuming a lot of sugar and drinking a lot of soft drinks and a higher rate of ADHD diagnoses, other research does not discover any connection at all. Even if it does not help improve ADHD symptoms, restricting sugar intake is a healthy decision for everyone because it may reduce the risk of diabetes, obesity, and tooth decay. This is true even if it does not help improve ADHD symptoms.

Other simple carbohydrates

Sugar is a refined form of carbohydrate. Other simple carbs can also contribute to rapid variations in blood sugar levels; thus, it is important for people to limit their consumption of foods high in simple carbohydrates as much as possible.

Although this is not a conducive list, the foods below contain simple carbohydrates:

- white bread
- candy
- potatoes without skins
- sports drinks
- white pasta
- potato fries
- soda
- white rice

Caffeine

Some studies suggest that caffeine might boost levels of concentration, so consuming moderate amounts of it can be beneficial for some people who have ADHD. Caffeine, on the other hand, has been shown to amplify the effects of certain ADHD drugs, including the likelihood of the user experiencing unwanted side effects. Adults diagnosed with ADHD should cut back on their caffeine consumption, especially if they are taking medication to treat their condition. Tea, coffee, and cola are all beverages that young children and teenagers should never drink.

Artificial Additives

Eliminating artificial additives from the diets of some children diagnosed with ADHD has been shown to be beneficial. Because they can make ADHD symptoms worse, certain chemicals, particularly food colorings, are something that the American Academy of Pediatrics (AAP) advises parents to keep their children away from.

Additionally, artificial chemicals have the potential to disrupt hormone balance, growth, and development. Many prepackaged and processed products, including some of the ones you buy at the grocery store, have artificial coloring, tastes, and preservatives:

- breakfast cereals
- candies
- cookies
- soft drinks
- fruit punches
- vitamins

Allergens

Some experts believe that avoiding foods that could cause allergic reactions, such as gluten, wheat, and soy, can help enhance concentration and lower hyperactivity levels. However, it is likely that the only people who will benefit from removing these allergens are those who genuinely have an allergy or sensitivity. Before cutting out certain foods completely from your diet, you might want to have a conversation about food allergies with a medical professional or a dietitian.

Cognitive Behavioral Therapy

This method places more of an emphasis on the thoughts and patterns of behavior that are causing you troubles in the here and now as opposed to any experiences that you may have had in the past. If you or your loved one has attention deficit hyperactivity disorder, they may have had more than a little exposure to undesirable beliefs and cognitive patterns that

- affect concentration or ability to focus.

- derail motivation and productivity.

- get in the way of things you want to do.

The goal of cognitive behavioral therapy (CBT) is to teach specific strategies for addressing harmful ideas and beliefs and promoting beneficial changes in behavior. CBT can teach these strategies.

Cognitive behavioral therapy is a pragmatic form of therapy that examines the ways in which our thoughts, feelings, and behaviors are molded not just by our own preconceived conceptions, but also by the world in which we find ourselves. The purpose of cognitive behavioral therapy (CBT) is to teach individuals how to recognize irrational thought patterns that contribute to undesirable behavioral outcomes and to teach them how to develop new thought patterns that are sensible in their place.

Benefits of CBT for Adults with ADHD

CBT is effective in treating many of the ADHD's peripheral symptoms, such as procrastination and difficulties managing both time and tasks. During a CBT session, the therapist develops a treatment plan for an adult patient with ADHD that considers these issues and works on the aforementioned aspects of daily functioning. The tasks might range from ensuring that financial obligations are met to encouraging activities that contribute to an individual's sense of well-being, such as getting enough sleep, exercising, and participating in hobbies.

Psychoeducation is an essential component of the treatment process because developing an awareness of individual symptoms can frequently facilitate the development of more effective coping strategies. The therapist you see will

- describe key ways it can affect thoughts, emotions, and behavior.

- explain more about ADHD.

- explain the process of therapy.

Behavior Modification

The process of behavior modification involves locating and eradicating any undesirable behaviors, as well as encouraging and establishing new behaviors that are more appropriate. Changing a child's behavior often necessitates the participation of the child's parents in the treatment process. The parents and the therapist collaborate on the development of a game plan for altering the child's behavior, which is subsequently carried out by the parents in their own home. Because children frequently struggle with the same difficulties of conduct at school, collaboration with teachers can also be beneficial.

Positive Self-Talk

It is quite common to berate yourself when you do not meet your goals, but doing so can also fuel feelings of worry, sadness, and self-hatred. If you want to feel better, try to avoid talking negatively to yourself. You will learn, as part of cognitive behavioral therapy (CBT), how to avoid negative self-talk and adopt positive messages that inspire self-compassion and kindness. Not only can positive self-talk make you feel more driven to stick to your objectives and complete chores, but it can also assist in minimizing the negative emotions that arise whenever you are confronted with adversity.

Skills Training

CBT offers skills training, an opportunity that addresses difficult but essential life skills. These include lessons in areas such as:

- navigating distractions
- time management
- developing adaptive thinking skills
- organizational skills
- setting smart goals
- reducing procrastination behaviors
- social skills
- psychoeducation
- making healthy lifestyle adjustments

Cognitive Restructuring

Cognitive restructuring breaks down negative thinking patterns by recognizing irrational ideas and replacing them with reasonable thoughts. Identifying irrational thoughts is the first step toward accomplishing the goal of cognitive restructuring. Even while this may not seem like an essential component of a treatment plan for ADHD, many people who have ADHD also have co-occurring issues such as depression, low self-esteem, or anxiety, which can make it more difficult to treat ADHD. That is where cognitive restructuring swoops in to save the day! It helps individuals retrain their brains to see themselves and their surroundings in a more constructive and positive light.

CBT and Results

The individual receiving treatment and the variety of symptoms they experience will determine how quickly they get effects from cognitive behavioral therapy (CBT). The typical course of treatment for cognitive behavioral therapy (CBT) consists of 10 to 12 sessions, with one session per week lasting for one hour. Depending on underlying mental health conditions or previous traumatic experiences, it may take some time before you start to see effects. It is essential to approach therapy with an open mind and complete the tasks your therapist assig s if you want to see improvements in a timely manner.

The treatment of ADHD that has traditionally been held in the highest regard consists of a combination of medication and talk therapy. Depending on the co-occurring mental health conditions, such as depression, anxiety, or PTSD, various modalities of cognitive behavioral therapy (CBT), such as mindfulness-based CBT and motivational CBT, can have an impact that is larger than that of classic CBT. In general, both medication and CBT are effective treatments for ADHD; however, research has shown that the combination of the two is the most beneficial.

How Effective Is CBT?

When people with ADHD were treated with a

combination of cognitive behavioral therapy (CBT) and medication, it was found that their condition improved significantly more than when they were treated with medication alone, according to the findings of a number of studies. It was discovered that these findings are accurate for children, adolescents, and adults who have been diagnosed with ADHD. (Corbisiero et al., 2018)

A study conducted in 2016 with forty-six adolescents who were on medication for ADHD investigated the benefits of cognitive behavioral therapy (CBT). According to the findings, cognitive behavioral therapy (CBT) may be an effective method for treating ADHD symptoms that do not appear to be helped by medication. (Sprich et al., 2016)

A meta-analysis conducted in 2018 looked at 14 trials of poor to moderate quality that explored the potential benefits of CBT as an ADHD treatment. The authors of the review stated that cognitive behavioral therapy (CBT) was useful in lowering hyperactivity, inattention, and impulsivity. They also discovered that a combination of cognitive behavioral therapy (CBT) and medication were more useful than medication alone for lowering anxiety and depression and enhancing day-to-day function.

A randomized clinical trial for adults with SUD and ADHD reported that after 15 CBT therapy sessions for adults with ADHD and SUD, their ADHD symptoms and substance use reduced.

Chapter 7:

What Pharmaceutical Treatment Options Are Available for Adult ADHD?

There is a wide variety of pharmaceutical therapy options available for adults who have been diagnosed with attention deficit hyperactivity disorder. The precise symptoms, as well as the degree of severity of the ailment, will determine the sort of medication one's care provider prescribes. Everyone reacts differently to the medicine used to treat ADHD. While some people see a significant improvement, others report feeling little to no relief. The adverse consequences manifest differently in different people for a variety of reasons. People must never take ADHD medication without first obtaining a doctor's prescription and they should always have strict supervision. Healthcare providers will adjust the dosages of the medication based on everyone's need and the following four factors:

- Duration of that medication.

- Optimal delivery system that best fits the individuals' needs, lifestyle, and insurance.

- Optimal molecule as a unique individual.

- Optimal dose that gives the best performance without side effects.

When addressing potential ADHD medication, it is important for individuals to be transparent about any other substances, prescriptions, or medications they are currently taking.

Common ADHD Medication

Although treating symptoms does not cure ADHD, how people deal with it now has changed from how they did ages ago. People with ADHD have a range of medications to choose from. If you or your loved one needs medication, their mental health professional will provide advice on common ADHD medication and their side effects.

Stimulant Therapies

Often referred to as psychostimulants, these pharmacologic medications are the first line of treatment for adult ADHD. They have a lengthy history and a moderate to substantial effect. Their tolerability and overall safety are good, especially when compared to most psychiatric medicines. As is to be expected with forms of treatment, stimulants also have side effects. However, when we account for their positive effects on working or driving, there is an even greater improvement in safety. To avoid being frustrated, it is advisable to begin taking the stimulants at a low level while adjusting up to the required level. Stimulants operate by boosting the levels of two chemicals in the brain called norepinephrine and dopamine. These chemicals play important functions in thinking and paying attention while also helping to reduce hyperactivity and impulsive behavior. Examples of the several classes of stimulants that are now on the market include derivatives of methylphenidate and amphetamine. Stimulants can have either a short or a long duration of action.

Short-Acting Stimulants

An individual can take these several times a day.

The most prescribed methylphenidate options include:

- Methylin liquid
- Focalin
- Ritalin

The amphetamines that healthcare workers most commonly prescribe include:

- Zenzedi (dextroamphetamine)
- Adderall (l'amphetamine-dextroamphetamine)
- Evekeo (amphetamine)
- Dexedrine Procentra / Zenzedi (dextroamphetamine)

- Desoxyn (methamphetamine)

Long-Acting Stimulants

These forms of stimulants simplify treatment regimens by enabling once-daily dosing, are more effective than short-acting preparations and are less likely to be abused or diverted from their intended purpose. Their pharmacokinetic characteristics lessen the dramatic onset and offset effects, which can either make patients uncomfortable or on occasion lead to overuse.

Common long-acting methylphenidates include:

- Cotempla XR
- Metadate CD
- Concreta
- Ritalin LA/XR
- Focalin XR
- Daytrana

Long-acting amphetamines include:

- Adderall XR (levoamphetamine and dextroamphetamine)
- Vyvanse (lisdexamfetamine)
- Mydayis (dextroamphetamine and levoamphetamine)
- Adzenys ER/Dyanavel XR

Although long-acting medications are not flexible, they are dependable. Individuals who are in good condition can make up for this lack of adaptability by topping off their dose with a small quantity of a short-acting drug in the evening if they need to study, drive, or work on demanding projects. Although these medicines are almost always consumed in the form of a pill, some of them can also be found in patch or liquid form.

Ritalin is a type of methylphenidate that has a rapid onset of action and wears off after around three to four hours. People who require immediate relief from their symptoms can benefit from using this medication. It takes effect quite rapidly, between 30 and 60 minutes, and is successful in treating over 70% of patients. Individuals who have noticeable anxiety, motor tics, a family history of Tourette syndrome, or a history of substance misuse should use it with caution. However, it should not be used in patients who have glaucoma because it is not safe for them to do so.

There is also a version of methylphenidate called Focalin, which has a duration of about four hours. After consuming it, you should begin to feel its effects within 30–60 minutes. When taken in the evening, when the effects of a longer-acting dose are starting to wear off, it operates more effectively. In patients who have a previous history of substance dependence, it is administered with extreme caution.

A combination of Ritalin SR, Methylin ER, and Metadate ER. These are medications with a moderate duration of action, and the onset of their effects may be delayed by anywhere from 60 to 90 minutes. Their duration is meant to be between 6 and 8 hours, although it can be quite individual and inconsistent. However, because it wears off more slowly than short-acting medications, there is less risk of rebound. If the pill is broken up or crushed, the complete dose may be released all at once, which would result in an overdose of two times the prescribed amount during the first four hours.

Both Ritalin LA (containing 50% delayed-release beads and 50% immediate-release beads) and Metadate CD (containing 70% delayed-release beads and 30% immediate-release beads) are mild-acting stimulants, with an onset time of between thirty minutes and an hour and a duration of about eight hours. If the beads are chewed, the full dose may be released all at once, and the entire contents may be consumed during the first four hours.

Concreta, which contains 78% delayed release and 22% immediate release, is one of the methylphenidate drugs that has one of the longest effects on the market, since its effects can last anywhere from 10 to 14 hours. It only needs to be taken once a day, in the morning, and its cutting-edge formula kicks in within 30 to 60 minutes, with peak levels reaching their maximum after 6 to 10 hours. The medication is progressively delivered throughout the day, so there is no possibility of a midday gap or a rebound. Additionally, because it wears off gradually than short-acting medications, there is less rebound and a lesser risk of misuse.

Short-acting versions of amphetamines include Evekeo, Adderall IR, Dexedrine, and Zenzedi. These amphetamines begin to take effect thirty to forty-five minutes after being taken, and they continue to be effective for a period of four to five hours. In general, the effects of amphetamines are comparable to those of methylphenidate, even though amphetamines tend to be slightly more powerful than methylphenidate and to last a little bit longer.

Adderall XR is a good example of a drug that has an extended release (XR), which is preferred over treatments with a rapid onset of action. The extended-release formulation of Adderall, known as Adderall XR, has a pill that dissolves more gradually than regular Adderall, allowing the body to gradually absorb the medication. The longer-acting version of Adderall, known as Adderall XR, has an effectiveness window of 10 to 12 hours and is only required to be taken once a day, but the immediate release version, known as Adderall IR, can be consumed anywhere from one to three times daily. Around eighty percent of patients benefit from the use of stimulants. Long-acting formulations are more effective than short-acting preparations because they allow for uncomplicated treatment regimens to be carried out once daily.

ADHD stimulants may do the job for many individuals but are not for everyone. They are not recommended for individuals with:

- Psychosis, or a history of the condition.
- A build-up of fluid pressure in the eyes, known as glaucoma.
- Underlying heart problems.
- Recurring, uncontrollable body movements, also called tics.

- Severe anxiety or agitation.

- Tourette's syndrome, or a family history of it.

The same applies for an individual who has taken a form of medication called a monoamine oxidase inhibitor within two weeks. Examples of monoamine oxidase inhibitors include tranylcypromine (Parnate) and phenelzine (Nardil).

Central nervous system stimulants are also not recommended for people who take too much alcohol or other medications that have alcohol. This is because the combination with certain long-acting stimulants can cause a serious interaction. With such interactions, the medication would be released into the system too quickly, and that can lead to harmful side effects or even an overdose.

Non-Stimulants

After the first line of treatment for ADHD come non-stimulant therapies. These second line of adult ADHD pharmacotherapy options may be used as:

- Independent therapy options for individuals who cannot receive stimulant therapy.

- Treatment for comorbid anxiety or depression where there is room to directly deal with symptoms of ADHD as well.

- Treatment argumenters in combination with stimulants.

The effect of non-stimulants on symptoms of ADHD is often not as great, but these treatments have lasting benefits, fewer regulatory limitations, and less possibility for diversion. On top of all that, non-stimulants are also the options that have less of a stigma attached to them.

Certain antidepressants such as SNRIs, agomelatine, and bupropion have a few traces, but may still deliver the same effect. Atomoxetine (Strattera) is the most effective medication that does not use stimulants. It was the first medication to be approved by the Food and Drug Administration (FDA) for the treatment of attention deficit hyperactivity disorder.

Atomoxetine is effective because it works by increasing the amount of nor-epinephrine only, which is an essential chemical in the brain. This helps ADHD patients by enhancing their ability to focus for longer periods of time. One or two doses are to be taken each day, either with or without food. The treatment begins to take effect anywhere from a few days to a week, but the full effect may not be visible for at least a month. Duration all day, twenty-four hours a day, seven days a week, if it is taken regularly as advised. Because it does not cause euphoria or lead to abuse, it is not considered a prohibited drug, and those who have a history of abusing substances can use it too. However, patients who suffer from tachycardia, hypertension, or cerebrovascular or cardiovascular disease should use this medication with extreme caution.

Other non-stimulant drugs, such as alpha-2 adrenergic agonists like guanfacine and clonidine, have shown some evidence of being beneficial in the treatment of adult ADHD. Due to the lack of significance of the impact, it is only infrequently recommended to employ them as adjuncts. Clonidine begins to work in 30 minutes to an hour, and its effects usually last between 3–6 hours. It is beneficial for patients suffering from ADHD who also have a co-occurring tic condition or sleeplessness; also effective for treating extreme hyperactivity, impulsivity, or violence. Clonidine also stimulates appetite.

Guanfacine has a lesser sedative effect than clonidine, but its effects last for around 6-12 hours. The medication can modulate impulsivity and hyperactivity around the clock.

Antidepressant Medication Options for ADHD

Although the FDA has not given its approval for people to use any antidepressant in the treatment of ADHD, most medical professionals will recommend one of the following medications:

Wellbutrin: The average duration of action of Wellbutrin IR is between four and six hours. It is helpful for ADHD patients who also have a comorbid depression or anxiety disorder, but it is not indicated in individuals who have a seizure disorder or who have a current or previous diagnosis of bulimia or anorexia. Patients with ADHD who also have a comorbid depression or anxiety disorder benefit from it. Long-acting Wellbutrin SR has a duration of 10 to 14 hours and a decreased seizure risk compared to the quick-release variant of the medication. Wellbutrin XL is a long-acting antidepressant that has a duration of 24 hours or more, a single daily dose, and a decreased risk of seizure. Inhibitor of norepinephrine-dopamine reuptake is the purpose that Wellbutrin serves in the body. This indicates that it helps enhance levels of dopamine and norepinephrine in the brain, both of which contribute to improved attention, hyperactivity, and other symptoms associated with ADHD.

Effexor (venlafaxine): This medication is a serotonin and norepinephrine reuptake inhibitor (SNRI), which means that it increases the levels of serotonin and norepinephrine in the brain.

Benefits of ADHD Medications

Medication for attention deficit hyperactivity disorder (ADHD) can reduce symptoms in approximately 70% of adult patients. They tend to be less hyperactive, less likely to interrupt, and less likely to fidget. People that suffer from ADHD will benefit from having:

- reduced impulsivity

    o People living with ADHD who take their medication as they should often do not interrupt others while they are talking, behave in socially inappropriate manners, rush through tasks, or do things without carefully considering the possible consequences.

- improved relationships

  - With proper medication, people who have ADHD start getting along with coworkers, having less disputes with others, and improving communication with their families and friends. These are all steps toward achieving this goal. From this perspective, we can also say that ADHD medication promotes a decline in the number of marriages that end in divorce.

- reduced forgetfulness

  - Because ADHD medications lower the risk of forgetfulness, people with ADHD are better able to recall key dates and appointments, ensuring that their condition does not hinder their professional lives.

- improved quality of life

  - Taking medicine for ADHD will enhance an individual's quality of life by reducing the likelihood of experiencing depression and anxiety, as well as lessening the frequency with which one consumes alcohol or drugs.

- reduced anger outbursts

  - Because ADHD medications assist patients to gain emotional control, those with ADHD are less likely to lose their cool over insignificant issues.

- increased road safety

  - Taking ADHD medication as advised promotes a decreased likelihood of receiving speeding fines, protection against having one's license suspended, and reduces untimely deaths brought on by accidents.

- the ability to prioritize issues

  - Attention deficit hyperactivity disorder patients can prioritize problems and fulfill significant commitments.

- increased employment

  - Individuals living with ADHD who have more employment opportunities and take their medicine will have an easier time getting to work on time, finishing their work by the deadlines they'vethey have set, being organized, and taking constructive criticism in stride.

- reduced suicide

  - Less people commit suicide because of taking ADHD medication because it helps improve their negative hypercritical self-image and makes them less likely to regard challenges as personal failures or underachievement.

Possible Side Effects

There is always the possibility of adverse consequences when taking medication. Not everyone will have the same negative effects, if any at all, from taking this medication. It is possible that some of the negative effects will not go away, while others will.

- seizure or irregular heartbeat

  - Atomoxetine has been known to cause both seizures and cardiac irregularities, so take caution if you have any of these conditions.

- mood changes

  - A stimulant dose that is too high can create drowsiness, impatience, or tearfulness in the individual taking it. Altering the amount of medication taken at each dose is one solution to this problem. Some individuals are susceptible to experiencing shifts in their mood when they take stimulants, regardless of the amount. When people quit using the stimulant, this problem goes away. Sometimes switching to a different stimulant prescription can be helpful, but other times it is required to take a drug that is not a stimulant to treat the mood swings.

- cardiac effects

  o Most people with ADHD experience a rise in their blood pressure and heart rate when they use psychostimulants like cocaine or amphetamines. This does cause some issues on occasion. Stimulants can elevate resting blood pressure by five to ten points, which means that those who already have borderline high blood pressure may discover that they need to begin taking anti-hypertensive medication as a result of taking the stimulant. People who already have cardiac rhythms that are not normal can discover that the modest rise in pulse rate causes some complications for them. The issue may be addressed by utilizing lesser dosages or by combining different medications to find a solution.

- sleep problems

    - It is possible for medicine used to treat ADHD to disrupt sleep, and this is especially true if the medication is still active at bedtime. It is possible that the second or third dose of a short-acting prescription is being taken too late in the day, in which case the effects of the first dose have not yet worn off.

- psychiatric problems

    - The possibility of a link between ADHD medications and mental health problems seems remote, though. For instance, some individuals have reported experiencing behavioral issues such as belligerence and anger. Others claim that they started exhibiting indications of bipolar disorder.

    - The Food and Drug Administration has issued a warning that there is a possibility that stimulant ADHD medications could cause symptoms of psychosis, such as hearing voices and experiencing paranoia.

- eye problems

    - Any drug that contains a stimulant will also slightly raise the eye pressure. It is possible that people who have glaucoma are more sensitive to even a minor elevation in pressure. Because of this, the drug should be stopped immediately whenever a person is experiencing severe eye pain. If a person is taking stimulants and experiences blurred vision while taking them, they should not stop taking the prescription because the side effect typically goes away within a few weeks.

- stimulation side effects

    ○ Some people who use stimulants report experiencing side effects such as feeling wired, jittery, worried, or having heart palpitations. In most cases, this indicates that the dose is too high, that it is being taken too frequently, or that the individual is receiving additional stimulation from other substances such as caffeine.

- headaches

    ○ As the medicine leaves the body, there is typically an increase in the number of headaches experienced by the patient. This typically occurs at the very end of the prescribed dosage. Moving the dosages in closer proximity to one another may provide relief from the headaches. People who have a personal or family history of vascular headaches (migraines) are more likely to experience more severe headaches that last throughout the entire dose of the medication. These headaches can typically be cured entirely by using a calcium channel blocker medicine for a relatively short period of time.

- gastrointestinal disturbances

  - Medications that are classified as stimulants can create gastrointestinal issues, which can make it difficult to eat. The stimulant drug is active and suppresses the appetite, but it may only look like the person is not eating because they are not hungry. When taking medicine for ADHD, some people find that they lose their appetite, which in turn causes them to lose weight. If one has cramps, taking the drug with food is helpful in treating the condition. Constipation of a milder nature may also be observed; however, this side effect typically disappears after a few weeks have passed. One of the most prevalent negative effects is a loss of appetite.

The following are specific ADHD drugs with some of their common side effects:

- Ritalin, Methylin, Metadate, Focalin, Adderall, and Adderall XR

  - decreased appetite

- insomnia
- weight loss
- irritability
- rebound agitation or exaggeration of pre-medication symptoms
- headache
- stomachache

- **Atomoxetine**
  - dry mouth
  - anxiety
  - sleep problems
  - fatigue
  - dizziness
  - upset stomach

- **Clonidine and Guanfacine**
  - low blood pressure
  - dizziness
  - fatigue
  - dry mouth
  - behavior problems
  - crankiness

ADHD medication may also cause tremors or an increase in involuntary muscular twitches termed tics.

Because tics normally wax and wane, the tic may usually go away on its own without medical intervention. However, if an individual removes coffee from their diet, more than half of the symptoms of tics will disappear, and that brings us to our last section in this chapter.

Interactions With Other Medications

Fewer drugs interact with psychostimulant medications than with other types. A person who is currently under the influence of psychostimulants or pharmaceuticals should avoid the following:

- steroids

    o If you are taking stimulant medication for ADHD while also receiving steroid treatment, you are required to stop taking steroids immediately, regardless of whether you are injecting them or taking them orally.

- cold, sinus, or hay fever medications

    o Drugs for the common cold, sinusitis, and hay fever have decongestants. Decongestants are moderate stimulant medications that we use for their capacity to dry mucus. These will make the negative effects that have previously been present more worse.

- caffeine

    - Caffeine-containing beverages (such as coffee, tea, and red bull) and excessive amounts of chocolate have the potential to cause jitteriness in some people.

- nicotine-containing products

    - Products that contain nicotine will cause a sharp increase in both your blood pressure and your heart rate. Early studies revealed that nicotine and several of its analogs have some slight benefits for ADHD; however, these benefits are exceeded by the severe effects of tobacco use for the cardiovascular system and for cancer.

We will cover more on drug interactions in the following chapter.

Chapter 8:

What Substances Interact

with My ADHD Medications?

Stimulants are the most common pharmacological treatment of attention-deficit hyperactivity disorder. ADHD is characterized by symptoms such as having trouble paying attention, being extremely active, and behaving without thinking about the repercussions of one's actions, and that is where stimulants work their magic. However, because stimulants boost a person's ability to pay attention, stay alert, and maintain elevated levels of energy, these drugs can also be used to treat a variety of other neurological and mental health issues. For instance, medical professionals can administer stimulants to patients who suffer from narcolepsy to prevent them from having unexpected episodes of sleepiness.

Attention deficit hyperactivity disorder medications interact with different substances which affect their effectiveness and cause serious side effects. Substances that interact and interfere with the role of ADHD drugs are:

- drugs such as antidepressants
- alkalinizing agents

- steroids

- caffeine

- nicotine

- asthma

- medication

- guanethidine

- reserpine

- certain opioids

- alcohol

- citrus fruits

- nutritional supplements that contain vitamin C

- high vitamin cereals

Remember that the negative interactions occur when one substance causes another to have a different effect than expected. Everyone has their own unique approach to making the most of their free time, and for many people, this includes indulging in some pleasures that may include alcohol. If you or your loved one has a big day coming and alcohol is going to be the heart of the party, you will have to consider possible drug interactions before the fun begins. Is it wise to combine alcohol consumption with the taking of medication for ADHD? What are the dangers of drinking alcohol if you have not gotten treatment for the condition?

Alcohol Interaction with ADHD Medication

Even the packaging of ADHD medications discourages individuals from drinking alcohol. However, there are medical professionals who believe it is okay for patients to consume a beer or two. When combined with alcohol, many stimulants can produce a variety of adverse effects on the cardiovascular system as well as the central nervous system. It is possible for individuals to experience symptoms such as dizziness, drowsiness, decreased focus or coordination, seizures, depression, and anxiety. Driving or operating machinery in such a state could put one's life in danger because they may not know what they can and cannot handle. When one combines alcohol and their ADHD medication, the two fail to reach the desired balancing effect on one another. The relaxed and intoxicating sensation that comes from drinking alcohol can be lessened by taking medication for ADHD. As a result, an individual runs the risk of drinking more than they should, which could cause alcohol poisoning.

When alcohol is used with amphetamine derivatives, there is an increased potential for cardiovascular side effects such as a high heart rate, chest pain, and even a heart attack. If you or your loved one has a history of heart disease, they should specifically avoid alcohol or any drugs that contain compounds. You should also tell your healthcare practitioner if you have a history of abusing drugs or alcohol at any point in your life.

Combining alcohol and some long-acting stimulants such as Ritalin LA or Metadate CD, which are both prescribed to treat attention deficit hyperactivity disorder (ADHD), may result in a dangerous interaction. In most cases, it is best to abstain from drinking when under the influence of a long-acting stimulant. Consuming alcohol raises the risk of the medicine entering the body at an accelerated rate, which increases the risk of potentially harmful side effects and even an overdose.

Antidepressants Interaction with ADHD Medication

- monoamine oxidase inhibitors (MAOIs)

  - While taking ADHD drugs, it is not safe for an individual to start taking MAOIs. MAOIs such as selegiline, isocarboxazid, and linezolid can have an interaction effect with ADHD stimulant medications like Amphetamine, and Adderall. If one must take MAOIs, it is crucial that the individual ensures 14 days in between. If not, severe side effects can occur. MAOIs like ADHD drugs also increase the heart rate and blood pressure, which can lead to hypertension (a dangerous increase in blood pressure), stroke, or even a heart attack. This drug combination can also cause build-up of the chemical substance in the body called serotonin which can lead to mild shivering and diarrhea to severe muscle stiffness, fever, and seizures.

- selective serotonin reuptake inhibitors (SSRIs)

  - Examples of SSRIs are fluoxetine, sertraline, citalopram, and paroxetine. Using sertraline can amplify the effects of ADHD medication such as amphetamine. Sertraline can also increase the adverse effects of those medications, including anxiety, nervousness, restlessness, and racing thoughts. The combination of these medications can risk the individual to an increase in the levels of serotonin too just like the MAOIs and the TCAs, which can result in coma and death, if the serotonin levels are too high.

- tricyclic antidepressants (TCA)

  - These include Amitriptyline, Desipramine, and Imipramine also interact with ADHD drugs. The absorption of Atomoxetine can be decreased. When combined with Amitriptyline which will lead to less effectiveness on the treatment of ADHD. Interaction with Adderall can increase the risk of serotonin syndrome which can cause dry mouth, dilated pupils, hallucinations, delirium, high body temperature, and sweating more than usual.

Apart from the antidepressant drugs, other medications that interact with ADHD drugs include the following such as acid-reducing drugs. Examples of acid-reducing drugs include antacids and omeprazole. These act by reducing acid in the stomach and are used to treat heartburn and stomach ulcers, when they interact with ADHD drugs like Adderall, they increase the level of Adderall in the body, which will increase the side effects of the drug. An individual will experience a fast heart attack, overdose, stroke, severe headache, mood swings, depression, sexual dysfunction, insomnia, and increased blood pressure.

Caffeine Interaction with ADHD Medication

Some people grab cups of coffee to help them through the day, while others make it their go-to beverage for stressful times. Caffeine is a popular substance throughout the world, and can be found in beverages such as coffee, tea, and chocolate. But then, what effects does it have on your brain? If you consume too much coffee, it may cause you to feel jittery, agitated, or angry. However, consuming just the perfect amount can help you focus.

Because caffeine is so widely consumed, it is essential to understand the effects that it has on people living with ADHD. Caffeine is a stimulant that energizes the central nervous system of the body by increasing the production of a neurochemical called dopamine in the brain. This substance is responsible for regulating one's ability to focus and retain concentration. A person who is stimulated by new information. When an individual stimulates their mind at their level, they have energy as well as a diminished sensitivity to the negative consequences of exhaustion. However, that is not the entire story; the result of taking coffee is not always favorable. Caffeine can cause even more severe sleep disruptions or insomnia in individuals who already have difficulties falling or staying asleep. That then makes it difficult for people with ADHD to perform activities when they need to.

The effects of consuming coffee on ADHD are still primarily based on anecdotal evidence. Some people find that the stimulant makes them feel calmer, but others report that it makes them feel more anxious. On the other hand, several parents and adults who have ADHD testify that light to moderate caffeine usage is an effective strategy to assist enhance focus and concentration.

The use of stimulants will, in most cases, cause agitation and anxiety by driving dopamine levels to unsafely elevated levels. However, the addition of stimulants can help those who have ADHD achieve the optimal levels. Consuming many cups of coffee at various points throughout the day rather than gulping it all down at once makes a significant effect when trying to focus.

Caffeine, according to the findings of several research, can help individuals with ADHD improve their concentration. Because it is a stimulant drug, it has some of the same effects as higher stimulants such as amphetamine drugs that are used to treat ADHD. However, as compared to prescription drugs, caffeine on its own is not as effective. Although it can be used to help relieve symptoms of ADHD in adults without risking their health, young children and teenagers should avoid it at all costs.

So, here is what you need to know about ADHD medication and caffeine: The effect that occurs when an individual takes caffeine and amphetamine-based medications, such as dextroamphetamine, together is called synergy. It happens when one takes two treatments that have different but complementary mechanisms of action at the same time. Drinking caffeine-containing beverages with amphetamine-based ADHD medications makes their combined effects more powerful. Given the fact that coffee boosts the efficacy of amphetamines, an individual who takes, say, Adderall, is likely to experience a more pronounced effect, as well as an increased risk of experiencing side effects.

Because coffee and most ADHD medications are both considered to be stimulants, it is possible that taking them together can put one at risk for having more serious adverse effects such as cardiac overstimulation. Although some people can drink coffee while also taking ADHD medication without any adverse effects, this capacity is highly dependent on the quantities of both chemicals.

When caffeine stimulates the body, it may lead to an individual having reduced sleep. The lack of adequate sleep can then cause ADHD-like symptoms. People with ADHD who take a lot of caffeine may encounter symptoms such as:

- Difficulty controlling emotions.
- Increased forgetfulness.
- Irritability.
- Trouble focusing or sitting still.

If you or your loved one has ADHD, they should limit their caffeine intake to the morning hours and avoid drinking coffee, chocolate, tea, or soda in the evenings or late at night.

Sleep deprivation is not the only problem with taking caffeine when one has ADHD. Too much caffeine may also cause rapid heartbeat, muscle shakes, or upset stomach. An individual who takes both caffeine and amphetamines receives a double dose of the adverse effects of each of these substances because pharmaceutical combinations are extremely difficult to manage. Anxiety, trouble sleeping, nausea, and stomach pains are all potential side effects of both medicines.

Vitamin C

Ascorbic acid, also known as vitamin C, is a water-soluble vitamin that can carry nutrients to the tissues of the body. However, because it does not store well, it must be consumed on a regular basis, either through food or nutritional supplements.

Vitamin C is a potent antioxidant that may fight off potentially dangerous free radicals. It also plays an important part in the prevention of infections and the healing of wounds. It is necessary to produce collagen, which is a fibrous protein found in connective tissue that is woven across many of the body's systems, including the neurological system, the immune system, bone, cartilage, and blood, among others. The vitamin is necessary to produce a number of hormones and chemical messengers that are utilized by the brain and the nerves.

So, does the vitamin affect your ADHD medication?

Yes. If you are taking medication for ADHD, avoid taking ascorbic acid or vitamin C an hour before or after taking the medication. Because stimulants have a high alkaline pH, it is impossible for them to be absorbed into the bloodstream while these organic acids are present.

Oranges, grapefruits, and vitamin C all contain acid, which inhibits the absorption of drugs used to treat ADHD. Adderall and Ritalin, which have a rapid onset of action. In addition, there are drugs with a prolonged effect, such as Vyvance and Concerta. This is because they begin with a boost that has a short duration of action, allowing it to swiftly stimulate your brain.

It is possible that taking a very high amount of vitamin C (1000 milligrams) in the form of a tablet or juice could hasten the excretion of the drug in the urine, causing it to leave your system too rapidly. When you take your medication, such as Adderall or Ritalin, you should not consume any fruit juices, including grapefruit juice or orange juice.

You do not have to stop drinking juice every day or taking your vitamin C supplement, but you should just hold off on taking your prescription for about an hour before and after you take it. By that time, the drug will have passed through your system to a point where the acid from the citrus will not have an effect on it.

Other Substances

Tobacco products that contain nicotine also interact with ADHD drugs, raise blood pressure and pulse rate, tobacco should be discontinued while on ADHD drugs.

Any food containing caffeine such as tea, coffee, chocolate, and cola drinks interact with ADHD drugs which increase ADHD drugs' side effects such as trouble sleeping, anxiety, and increased heart rate. Large amounts of food containing large amounts of caffeine should be avoided while taking ADHD drugs.

Remember that ADHD drugs interact with vitamin C and fruit juices containing citric acid such as cranberry juice, so if you enjoy partying with citric fruits, your medication may not function as it is supposed to. Some people living with ADHD forget or choose to ignore the fact that alcohol does not go well with their medication. However, it is crucial to remember that drinking alcohol can worsen your symptoms to an extent so serious you may never be able to take a sip of alcohol.

When you or your partner visits a mental health care specialist, the professional will take past medical history as well as personal habits and general abilities into account. That will help the experts know what treatment is best for the situation and advise further. Medication is one of the therapies for ADHD that is suggested to patients more often than any other medication. In addition to medicine, you may find that additional treatments, such as counseling for you and your family, behavioral therapy, and psychotherapy, are beneficial to you.

Chapter 9:

Can I Continue to Work

After My ADHD Diagnosis?

Having ADHD is not the end of your work life. Though the disorder is incurable and may affect your performance at work, it is treatable. Starting early treatment, therapy, support, and modifying your work habits will help you not only to manage your symptoms but also help you excel and have success in your work. It is not impossible to excel in your work once you dedicate time to take proper measures. Living with ADHD implies identifying and knowing your symptoms and actively finding what works for you and enables you to be able to carry out your duties effectively.

ADHD in Work Settings

ADHD is known as a neurological, developmental, and incurable but treatable lifelong disorder. It affects behavior, normal work of function, and one's ability to execute some tasks of life efficiently. ADHD in a work setting can present as inattentiveness to work, *time myopia*, also known as time blindness, executive function, sluggish cognitive tempo, and more. To help broaden the understanding of these manifestations in a workplace, have separately been explained below:

Inattentiveness

Inattentiveness manifests as the inability to pay proper attention to tasks at work. The person finds it difficult to concentrate and stay focused on the work task they are supposed to carry out. It impacts how a person delivers their abilities at work and may leave a mark on their reputation. The symptoms of inattentiveness can lead one to frustration, feeling of incompetence and low self-esteem, and subsequently depression. It is important to understand that though these symptoms may manifest in your work, there are tips that you can use and implement to counteract the manifestations of inattentiveness. The manifestations of inattentive and helpful tips have been listed and explained below:

- having difficulties paying attention to detail
  - They put little or no effort in ensuring that the task they are given is carried out with accuracy and precision and the objective of the task is met and lack the sense of priority. Because of this they frequently make errors and mistakes with work tasks and hence end up losing the trust of their employers which may eventually lead to them losing their job.

Tips

- Engage yourself in activities that help train, sharpen your focus, and increase your attention to detail. You can try solving puzzles or find other exciting memory tasks.

- Take regular breaks and rest because for your brain to process information properly it needs to have rested.

- Observe and get familiar with your work environment.

- Practice self-care by reducing activities or other interactions that cause you stress.

When you have ADHD, you can find yourself getting easily distracted by things that are unrelated to the work you have been assigned to work on, such as filling in work reports. A person without ADHD can easily redirect their mind from distractions unrelated to their work and hence they can focus on the work given and carry it out effectively. However, in a person with ADHD, it is more like they are not in control of the distraction and therefore find it hard to redirect their mind from the external or internal distractions such as noises, movement in the work environments, and objects. If you have ADHD and experiencing distractibility at your workplace, below are some tips that can be helpful :

- Discuss with your employer on the possibilities of giving you a private personal room to do your work from or find unused quiet places to work from such as the conference room, or request to do your work from home.

- If you are easily distracted by noise from your workplace, improvise the use of earphones, play some music that helps you focus e.g., soft calming music. This helps in toning down the noise that can be from your colleagues and keep your mind from wandering off.

- When working, redirect calls to voicemail and set a time when specified calls can be made.

Poor Organization Skills

They find challenges in multitasking and fail to cope with tasks hence they often delay starting or completing given tasks. They have trouble having their time organized, and their thoughts and tasks are given to them. This may result in late coming and missing work, and they may have a reputation of being unreliable. Because they are usually disorganized, they tend to be forgetful. They may forget meeting appointments or instructions given at work, fail to meet up deadlines, or lose important documents and information.

Tips

- Once you reach home, set out 15 minutes to organize your work. You can write them in your diary and allocate time to each task by setting an alarm for each task.

- Use a planner or download a task organizer to help you keep track of your work.

- Use sticky notes to jot down all tasks that you need to carry out.

- Every day write down a to-do list. It will help you in identifying where you are lagging and help keep track of your overall performance.

- Set reminders on your phone for any appointments.

- Put away any items that are unnecessary for tasks assigned.

- Find a specific place to store all your work-related files and information. It does not have to be an entire room; a small box or drawer will do.

- Arrange your files and other work materials in a neat, specified area that will make it easy for you to identify them when you need access.

Procrastination

To avoid missing deadlines, have them marked out boldly on your calendar or on your phone with the time for submission indicated. It can also manifest as difficulty to follow through on tasks and instructions. They avoid or dislike tasks that require sustained mental efforts such as large tasks with a prolonged duration and delayed rewards. Because of this, they easily get bored with tasks and fail to complete them and procrastinate.

Tips

- Divide your larger tasks into smaller ones and give yourself a reward for each task completed.

- Give yourself short breaks between tasks to avoid boredom. You can take a walk, watch a short video, and anything that you like.

- Take down important notes. Jot them in your diary or notepad and record important meetings. This will serve as backup information that you can reference when you start carrying out your work.

Poor Communication Skills

They find it difficult to concentrate on what a person is saying, it is not like they cannot communicate but they appear not to be listening when they are being spoken to, thoughts wandered into space and may therefore be termed as rude. In other instances when instructions for how work should be carried are given, those instructions often must be repeated to them because they either did not hear the instructions because of wandered thoughts (absent-mindedness) or they have forgotten.

Tips

- Implement active listening and practice paying attention. Maintain eye contact when communicating and keep your focus on the person giving you the information, for instance, your supervisor or workmate.

- Ask questions where you are not clear.

- Ask for advice on how you can improve and implement.

Sluggish Cognitive Tempo

It is also referred to as brain fog and it affects the alertness and speed at which one carries out their work. Its manifestation at work is listed and explained below:

- poor memory retrieval
    - A person with sluggish cognitive tempo will have a harder time remembering what they are taught at work meetings, how to carry out the specified instruction to their work or assignment, have poor listening skills and are inattentive to detail. They also have difficulties expressing their thoughts. These individuals tend to hide their emotions, and ideas because they are mostly afraid of facing criticism about their work abilities and performance.

Other manifestations of sluggish cognitive tempo at work include:

- acting withdrawn
    - They find it hard to connect socially with their colleagues, clients, and

employers hence they tend to withdraw.

- physical underactivity
- easily getting confused

Tips

- Always write down all important instructions or information specified for the work you ought to carry out down.

- Include exercise in your daily routines before starting out your work. This is because the part of your brain that is responsible for memory processing and retrieval of information is in the temporal lobe of the brain. Exercising helps improve blood supply to the temporal lobe and subsequently helps to keep your memory sharp.

- Have all your work organized.

Lethargic Behavior

Lethargy refers to a general state of fatigue. In a person with sluggish cognitive tempo, it implies the lack of motivation and interest to carry out their work duties (lack of mental or physical motivation). This subsequently leads to decreased alertness at doing work. People appear to be of low energy and are slower with tasks than usual and have impaired decision-making capacity and judgment. They may also manifest mood changes at work, for example, being irritable or short-tempered with their work colleagues. The other effect of lethargic behavior at work is that it reduces a person's awareness of their environment, memory relapses, and more.

Tips

- Engage in relaxing activities that trigger positivity. Do something that is not too relaxing on your body physically but gives you the chance to draw out positive energy that drives you to carry out your work duties.

- Create small goals and try to make your internal dialogue more pleasant i.e., motivate yourself by listening to motivational videos, and encourage yourself with positive words such as, "I can do this!"

- Remind yourself why you got employed, why did you choose to start work, and remind yourself of your goals

- Find your trigger, what helps build up interest in you to do work, it may be a book, taking a walk, or engaging in a sport.

- Give yourself time and be patient with your symptoms and do not compare yourself with others. You can find inspiration in how your colleagues do their work, but you must not look down on yourself. Acknowledge that if you are consistent in improving yourself, you will become better.

- Reach out for help. Do not be afraid or ashamed to ask or receive support. Reach out to a friend or close colleague at work who can give you the motivation to carry out your work duties when you are lacking in them.

Daydreaming

This implies that an individual's attention and focus drift away from their work to something entirely unrelated to what has been assigned to them. Daydreaming is constant. A person with sluggish cognitive tempo voluntarily spends more time daydreaming than attending to their work duties. The consequence of daydreaming is that it creates unproductivity and consumes enough time to disrupt their work responsibilities.

Tips

- Identify what drifts your attention and why you daydream and its patterns.

- Start training your thoughts to be grounded in the present. Counteract your daydreaming by focusing on something that is within your workspace that can help redirect your thoughts to the work you are carrying out. On the other hand, you can also do some simple exercises such as breathing in and out, you can take a few minutes to meditate.

Slowness in Processing Information

Processing information simply means the time it takes for a person to absorb and understand information and execute its intended function. A person with sluggish cognitive tempo finds it difficult to process work information given to them accurately and hence ending up making more errors and delaying and executing their required duties at work effectively. They struggle to plan out their work properly, have trouble understanding and following complex instructions, manage their time correctly, and start and finish tasks on time. This affects work performance as it reduces one's ability to perform work automatically when it is given and therefore brings about frustration and increases risks of anxiety and depression.

Tips

If you are struggling with processing information the tips below can be helpful :

- Avoid multitasking at work.
- Get plenty of aerobic exercises.

Time Myopia

It is also known as time nearsightedness. In a person with ADHD, this implies that they struggle and fail to plan because they don't see the future as clearly as a person without ADHD would. Time myopia in ADHD causes chronic procrastination.

Effective time management is essential in the making of long-term goals that are required for work and execution of function but because a person with ADHD struggles with time myopia they are usually inefficient with their workflow and low work quality.

Executive Dysfunction

It is also known as *function deficit* or the inability to carry out executive function skills. These execute functions include:

- working memory
  - This refers to the amount of information a person can hold in their mind to complete designated work tasks. A person with ADHD struggles with working memory retention and finds it difficult to hold enough information in working memory to feel sure of anything.

- flexibility and initiation
  - This means being able to plan for how work should be done, when to start or stop, and being able to think of all the steps of a task and arrange them in mind to see how to get from start to finish. People with ADHD however find it difficult to initiate tasks. They often start projects but may fail to finish the work. They are poor at planning and may feel overwhelmed by simple tasks.

Other manifestations of executive dysfunction at work may include:

- Having trouble keeping work appointments.
- May struggle with estimating the time each task

will take.

- Having trouble with planning for long-term work projects.

- Getting easily distracted from work.

- Having trouble listening and following up multi-step instructions.

- Having trouble keeping track of work-related possessions and often lose important work materials.

Tips

- When work has been assigned to you, ask for deadlines, or set one and work toward completing your work before the stated deadlines.

- Learn from your colleagues. Watch how others get started with their work and the steps they implement to have their work delivered effectively and on time. Then implement the strategies learned in your working plan

- Learn to encourage yourself. You can remind yourself every 15 minutes that you can do it to boost your motivation for work.

- Talk to yourself about the task or work that has been assigned to you. This will help you remember what you must do and when.

- Set reminders for meetings, and appointments and constantly remind yourself of the negative effects of procrastinating work e.g., losing your job.

- Always have enough rest.

Should You Tell Your Employer About Your ADHD Diagnosis?

Though most researchers discourage the thought of having to disclose your ADHD, you should know that the decision to conceal or reveal your ADHD diagnosis to your employer is up to you, and you are not obligated to tell them. It is important to understand that disclosing or concealing your diagnosis to your employer may come with either advantages or disadvantages and this may depend on:

- The amount of knowledge and awareness that your employer has on your diagnosis. Do they think it makes you incapable of working or do they understand you can still perform your duties?

- Your working environment and stipulated rules. How has your area of work responded to individuals who have tried to disclose their disorders? How were they treated? Is your area of work primed for disclosing your diagnosis?

- The relationship you have with your boss. Is it supportive or not?

- Another thought to put into considering when analyzing the idea of whether to disclose your diagnosis is knowing the why. What is the reason behind telling your employer about your diagnosis? Is it to play victim or provide information so that your employer has a better understanding of your diagnosis?

If you finally decide to tell your employer, here are a few tips you can implement when disclosing your diagnosis:

- Focus more on discussing challenges you face in your place rather than your ADHD diagnosis. This can help your employer to have a better understanding of the real challenges, and this may give a better chance for better outcomes. Be confident in your relaying of information but careful not to make your challenges an excuse for poor performance.

- Define your motive. Your reason to disclose your diagnosis should be to sensitize your employer and not play victim. It should not be a way to ask for favors regarding carrying out your work duties.

- Have a clear presentation of your ADHD with specific accommodation and productivity tools that can be implemented attached. After describing your struggles and challenges, outline a solution and the benefits it will bring, rather than leaving everything up to your employer.

Advantages of Disclosing Your Diagnosis

- Your employer may help offer you a working environment that helps you stay focused on work.

- It helps your employer and colleagues understand your challenges and how they can help you.

- You may also get protection from the law.

- Your employer may offer you an option to work from home.

Disadvantages of Disclosing Your ADHD Diagnosis

- You may receive discrimination if your employer lacks awareness on your diagnosis.

- It can risk you losing your job.

- Your employer or colleagues may think you are using your ADHD diagnosis as an excuse to poor work performance.

- It can cause you to be passed over for promotions.

- Your employer may treat you negatively and may influence the judgment of your employer on your overall work performance.

When Should You Disclose Your Diagnosis?

When you have implemented strategies and skills to help you function better at work and have failed and telling your employer may offer benefits that can help you execute your work functions effectively.

When Should You Not Disclose Your Diagnosis?

You can choose to conceal your diagnosis when the risks of disclosing your ADHD diagnosis to your employer are higher than the benefits. However, be sure to find and implement strategies, and skills that can help you have a better work performance in areas where you have challenges.

Examples of Successful ADHDers

Jamie Oliver

He is an award-winning British celebrity Chef, author and famous TV personality who was born in 1957. Jamie Oliver was awarded an MBE (Member of the Order of the British Empire) in the Queen's birthday honors. He disclosed his ADHD to the public, saying he got the diagnosis as a child. However, having ADHD did not hold him from being successful in life and work. His achievements are proof that you *can* succeed as an ADHDer!

Michael Phelps

Diagnosed with ADHD since childhood, he experienced attention difficulties and behavioral problems. However, Michael Phelps went on to become a swimmer and became an Olympic gold medalist swimmer and a notable example of a high achiever with ADHD.

Jay Carters

He is an employee who has worked at a 100-fortune company for 14 years. He was diagnosed with ADHD as a child, and experienced challenges keeping or sustaining a job as an adult. He saw himself bouncing from one job to another. However, things took a turn for him when he decided to raise awareness on ADHD by publishing his story in newspapers. He also disclosed his ADHD to his employer who showed understanding and implemented strategies to help Jay execute his job effectively. This saw Jaw carters working for 14 years effectively.

Duan Gordon

Diagnosed with ADHD at age 33, Duan Gordon suffered the challenges of being unable to sustain effective work function. From challenges in passing military school, to becoming a computer programmer who struggled with organization and attention, he went on to become a successful artist.

Lisa Ling

A successful journalist diagnosed with ADHD in 2014 at age 40. She explained that being diagnosed with ADHD pushed her to work even harder as a journalist. Apart from expert intervention she quoted and spoke about how having ADHD helped her to learn how to improve her work ethic. She learned to focus on subjects that excite her, and those she is passionate about.

Chapter 10:

Can I Drive and Operate

Machinery with Adult

ADHD?

Driving is a multifaceted activity that requires many different cognitive skills such as working memory, flexible thinking, and self-control to do well. It is believed that the underlying impairments that are characteristic of ADHD, such as the inability to pay attention, acting without thinking, and easily getting distracted, interfere with driving and lead to the development of undesirable consequences.

The cognitive impairments that are linked with ADHD in childhood extend throughout adulthood. However, relatively little is known regarding the influence that these challenges have on activities of daily life that are performed by adults, particularly in driving.

Adults who have been diagnosed with ADHD have been shown to have a significantly elevated incidence of both car accidents and driving-related legal problems. Adults with ADHD have a greater risk of the following:

- Losing focus while driving.

- Losing proper control of the vehicle.

- Exceeding the speed limit.

- Easily getting angry with other drivers on the road.

Adults with ADHD experience a greater decline in driving performance when under the influence of alcohol.

Cognitive deficiencies in ADHD have been demonstrated by a number of processes that may be responsible for poorer driving in this population. One such process is that people living with ADHD tend to be more distracted while driving. They might have problems with inhibitory motor control, lower levels of arousal, attentional lapses, and monitoring and evaluating performance, all of which are related to malfunction in the dopamine system. ADHD drivers are prone to the following errors such as:

- Ignoring speed limits.

- Not checking mirrors before changing lanes.

- Driving too close to the car in front.

- Not giving pedestrians chances to cross the road.

As mentioned earlier, inattention and impulsivity are hallmarks of ADHD. These behaviors may have their roots in a variety of causal chains and cognitive processes. Therefore, it is likely that these factors will also show to be relevant when individuals with ADHD are driving, and it is also possible that they may be able to predict certain elements of an individual's driving performance.

A failure to regulate arousal and motivational state is thought to be the cause of cognitive impairments in ADHD. Environmental elements that boost a person's drive might help lessen the cognitive deficits that ADHD causes. However, cognitive impairments worsen during long, boring cognitive tasks with low incentives. Contextual elements, such as the type of road and the environment around it, are known to influence driving in individuals who are healthy and may potentially influence driving performance in those who have ADHD. Driving on a highway may cause more driving errors in people with ADHD because of difficulties maintaining attention in low-stimulation environments. Activities such as failing to notice signs or hazards, and lane deviations, will be poorly performed. On the other hand, driving on urban routes may cause more driving violations (exceeding the speed limit, expressing verbal frustration with other drivers) because of an exacerbation of poor cognitive and emotional impulse control in a stimulating environment.

Significantly more people with ADHD are driving without licenses, having their licenses revoked or suspended, getting into many accidents, having a number of traffic fines, and particularly for going over the speed limit as compared to drivers who do not have ADHD.

When compared to drivers who do not have ADHD, those who do have ADHD are more likely to have negative opinions of their own driving habits. It is more likely for drivers who have ADHD to be legally at fault for traffic accidents than it is for drivers who do not have ADHD. When compared to drivers who do not have ADHD, those who do have the condition are more likely to be killed in a car accident and have more severe collisions. More than any other age group, adolescents are at a significant risk for being involved in an accident involving a motor vehicle. Teenage drivers who struggle with ADHD have a higher collision risk than their counterparts who do not have ADHD.

Medication for ADHD can significantly enhance one's ability to drive. However, additional work needs to be done to gain a better understanding of the underlying reasons and mechanisms that contribute to unsafe driving, as well as the treatments that can be used to improve safety.

Given what we know about the relationship between ADHD and driving, as well as the positive effects that medication can have on a person's ability to drive safely, it is essential to educate people living with ADHD and their families about the significance of safe driving, particularly if the person living with ADHD is a teenager or a young adult.

Safe Driving Advice for People Living with ADHD

- Get into the habit of active scanning.

  - When you are driving, you need to be aware of your surroundings, which includes knowing what is going on in front of you, behind you, and the lane next to you. Active scanning is the name given to this skill. If you are a caregiver and you are in the car with someone with ADHD, ask them to describe what is going on around you. This will assist them to develop this talent.

- Eliminate as many distractions as possible.

  - Even for inexperienced drivers, maintaining focus on the road can be challenging. When you include music, cell phones, and other passengers, it becomes much more difficult to concentrate.

  - Many state laws have limitations on the number and kinds of passengers that novice drivers can have in their vehicles. However, if you have ADHD, having restrictions apply for an even longer period or imposing further limitations can benefit your concentration.

- Always be adherent to your medication.

  - Make sure that any medicine you take for regulating your ADHD is still working, you should not miss a dose and you should take it as prescribed. This will improve your driving abilities and concentration when you are behind the wheel. Have a conversation with your doctor regarding driving. Inquire as to whether the dosage or timing needs to be altered for it to be effective while driving.

- Remain on paths that are already familiar to you.

  - People living with ADHD frequently have difficulty making plans and thinking about things in a variety of ways. Because of this, it is best to first stick to routes that are already familiar to you. This will help improve your concentration and improve your skills without having to worry about locating an alternative path.

- Make it a requirement to enroll in a recognized driver's education program.

  - This will help you learn more while interacting with others.

Chapter 11:

Where Can I Find Support and Resources for My Adult ADHD?

Apart from medical and therapy treatment for adult attention-deficit hyperactivity disorder, there are other steps to help support a loved one with Adult ADHD. The strategies have a notable and positive impact on both the individual with adult ADHD and their relationship with them. ADHD individuals can be supported by family support (parents, partners), workplace support, and support groups. Resources which help with ADHD include nonprofit organizations, blogs, books, and online communities.

Support for Adult ADHD

When I say you can survive a neurotypical world while living with ADHD, I do not mean you should do it alone—you should not have to. Most adults who have

ADHD manage to take control of their situations more when they receive support from the people around them, and the same applies to you. You should not be afraid or ashamed to seek help when you need a hand because craving support is part of being human.

Partner Support

ADHD affects relationships by causing misunderstanding and conflicts which can lead to separation or divorce. ADHD partners can help and support their partners without neglecting their own needs, they support their partners by:

- encouraging them to talk to a professional
    - Some ADHD individuals are not comfortable with the idea of therapy and may be hesitant to seek professional help, a partner can help by asking them about their reservations and try to explain to them the importance of therapy such as learning skills and coping strategies to better manage their condition, explore treatment options, practice communication skills this might encourage them to reach out. And whatever choice they make after explaining to them about professional help you totally support their decision, whether to seek it or not.

- emphasizing their strength
  - ADHD individuals have different strengths and time management is one of the challenges they face. Someone can be a fantastic, creative cook, but might have problems preparing dinner on time, they have a difficult time remembering specific details like which brand of tomato sauce the partner prefers. In such cases an ADHD partner can help support them by recognizing their area of strength like cooking, sharing the task more effectively, and appreciating their unique skill, such a statement like:
    - "I am looking forward to your cooking tonight."
    - "Is there anything I can help to get started with?"
  - This way, an ADHD individual will feel appreciated and encouraged to do the task on time.
- finding solutions for specific problems
  - When ADHD partners become aware of a problem, they should discuss it and collaborate to find a solution to it as soon as possible. For example, if the person with ADHD makes it a routine to pray or meditate whenever they have a little extra time before leaving for work, they are likely to become distracted and lose track of the passage

of time, which will cause them to be late for work. ADHD partners can bring out that problem and encourage them to set a reminder alarm before they start worshiping. If this strategy works, they can feel motivated to apply it to other situations on their own. But an ADHD partner should not always try to solve everything for them but only in specific situations because it sends the message that their partners do not believe that they can do anything for themselves.

- working on communication

  o ADHD individuals have poor communication, forgetfulness, and procrastination which can create problems in the relationship. ADHD partners can help and support them by communicating better with them not making it seem like it is their fault, tips for communication which can be used include:

    ■ listening to their side of things, after sharing your feelings, ask about their thoughts concerning what has been said.

    ■ mentioning concerns in a timely manner and sticking to the topic at hand instead of bringing up older issues this will help not create anger and resentment.

- ADHD partners should always remember that respect is the key, while asking them specific things or reminding them about important responsibilities, doing with consideration and kindness can help make a difference.

- figuring out what works for them

  - ADHD partners should support them by trying to find out what works for them instead of using specific strategies to explore specific available options together.

- practicing patience

  - ADHD individuals are emotionally drained with the responsibilities of work and daily life; they worry that their partners can give up and leave them if they keep messing things up. This can add stress and make it even harder for them to focus. ADHD partners can support them by practicing patience with them, asking them how they feel to have more insight into their day-to-day experience, this will make the ADHD partners understand them more and offer compassion instead of criticism.

Parent Support

Young adults with ADHD also need support from their parents. ADHD parents can help their children by:

- recognizing changes—even small ones

  - Many adult ADHDers struggle with self-awareness, they do not see how long it takes them to complete tasks, why they are consistently late or the impact their actions have on other people. Change requires recognition of behavioral and thought patterns. ADHD individuals may have a lot of careers, they may start a business that fails, attempt colleges that may not work out, or try jobs that do not fit. ADHD parents should encourage them and help them see how much they have accomplished and recognize anything they have done well.

- believing in them

  - ADHD individuals have difficulty making appointments, managing their finances, organizing things, and planning for the future. Despite the case, they try harder than those without ADHD, because they are lacking in so many executive functioning skills. Parents can support their adult ADHD children by believing them when they say they are trying and helping them realize when they may be stuck in a pattern. Help them try differently. When they are believed, it helps them build self-confidence and would not give up.

- helping them become their own advocates

  - ADHD parents can help their adult children with ADHD by speaking of empowerment, giving them the information they need, and encouraging them to make their own calls for job appointments.

- encouraging specialized ADHD help and training

  - ADHD professionals are trained to help ADHDers effectively plan their lives, get organized, manage their finances, use effective learning strategies, and make decisions. Parents make adults with ADHD understand the importance of professionals.

- helping them make decisions without influencing them

  - Parents can support their adult children with ADHD by allowing them to make their own decisions, not making decisions for them.

- helping them celebrate every success

  - Parents should help to celebrate with ADHD children whatever success they are making as this will make them feel more independent, happy, and they will make more effort towards achieving their goals. As a parent, be on the lookout for whatever step the ADHD child is making to be able to notice any decision made for desired results.

Workplace Support

Adults with ADHD have difficulties with concentrating and focusing which can lead them to lose their jobs, but they have the energetic drive and are able to hyper-focus on tasks that they are interested in, they are able to think holistically and make great leaders because of their resilience. There are different ways in which workmates and employers can support employees with adult ADHD and help them accomplish their tasks and feel accepted at the work.

Try:

- scheduling regular check-ins

  o Adults with ADHD have difficulties with time management, however, there are obstacles that might be getting in their way. ADHDers may miscalculate the amount of time they have until a deadline. Adults with ADHD can succeed when they have hard deadlines and are able to collaborate with their workmates on demanding tasks. They can stay on track by using regularly scheduled check-ins.

- supporting time management of projects and tasks

  o Adults with ADHD can be supported by confirming with an email showing projects with a timescale of when it must be completed, highlights of what needs to be done, why it has to be done and the desired outcome; and setting up a calendar inviting discussion with a reminder hours before. It will help the ADHD individuals with challenges with time and planning because of poor executive function.

- being sensitive and open-minded

  o Colleagues or employees with ADHD can be supported by getting to learn, understand, acknowledge them, and accept them. Workmates must be reliably consistent and not judge them. They need to be patient and sensitive toward individuals with ADHD.

- sharing more flexible ways to meet deadlines

  o Individuals with ADHD can receive support from their workmates if the coworkers share some strategies that can help ADHDers complete assignments on time. A brilliant example of such strategies is using a color-coded system to notate due dates so they can remember.

- helping them accomplish things done their own way

    o Encouraging them to stand up and move around in meetings or use fidget toys if it helps them to pay attention, in order to get things done not putting them under pressure and telling them how to perform their own task, this will make them feel confident enough and believe that they are trusted to do the work on their own.

- support by offering a switch of tasks when necessary

    o Adults with ADHD mostly feel diminished when they make mistakes regularly, ADHD can be helped by asking if they would like assistance by switching tasks, if they are not okay with the task they have been given, talking to them in a polite way not making them feel as if they are incapable.

- hiring an ADHD coach for support

    o Workmates can advise ADHD individuals about a Coach who will help them with building awareness, and develop strategies, to improve or eliminate performance gaps.

- encouraging them to join support groups

    o Support groups allow ADHD individuals to make friends with other people with ADHD. Support groups allow sharing of experiences, information, and coping strategies. These groups are available in person in many communities and online.

Resources for Adult ADHD

There are different resources for Adult ADHD where one can have information on attention deficit hyperactivity disorder and connect with other people who have ADHD. Resources include nonprofit organizations, blogs, books, and online communities.

Non-Profit Organizations

Some charities out there are willing to invest their time, resources, and energy into providing support for people who have ADHD. Examples of these include the following:

- CHADD
  - This is a national support organization that helps adults and children with ADHD. CHADD supports individuals who have ADHD with conferences, treatment options, and personal and adult online support communities. The organization also offers a resource directory, where individuals research for professionals in the area who may know

other support groups. It educates and advocates for individuals living with ADHD. CHADD publishes a variety of helpful materials and sends newsletters to members and professionals. The purpose of these publications is to ensure members and professionals have access to information about the latest research medications and treatments for people with ADHD.

- ADDA

  ○ Attention Deficit Disorder Associations, sometimes known as ADDA, is one of the most prominent ADHD charitable organizations in the world. This organization assists adults who have ADHD in having more fulfilling lives. It is a reliable resource, focusing solely on adult ADHD and related topics. Individuals from all walks of life are welcome in the group, and the organization has other groups that concentrate on workplace issues and support those who are subjected to stigma because of their unique way of thinking.

- American Psychiatric Association

  ○ One of the resources was a national medical specialty society with 3600 plus physical members who specialize in the diagnosis and treatment of emotional, mental, and substance abuse. Mental issues common with ADHD can be searched on this plate form. Psychiatrists can be located in the specific town an ADHD individual is on this site, other mental health problems like anxiety disorders, eating disorders and mood disorders can be found on this site.

- ADDitude Magazine Forum

  o This is an online magazine that covers recent events and findings linked to ADHD. It contains helpful information for individuals living with ADHD and those around them. It tackles a wide range of difficulties that may be experienced by individuals as well as their families, such as symptoms, diagnosis, and treatment.

- APSARD

  o American Professional Society of Attention Deficit Hyperactivity Disorder and Related Disorders, also called APSARD, improves results for individuals with ADHD and their families through promoting research throughout the lifespan on ADHD, and spreading based practices and education as evidence.

- American Speech-Language-Hearing Association

  o This resource is based on communication, it ensures effective communication which is accessible for all.

- National Institute of Mental health (NIMH)
    - The National Institute of Mental Health (NIMH) is a government body that provides comprehensive information regarding ADHD. You can use this to know about the symptoms, and statistics associated with the condition. NIMH also covers other aspects of mental health AND provides a list of clinical studies that are currently recruiting participants.

- Centers for Disease Control and Prevention (C.D.C)
    - C.D.C gives basic information about ADHD including its symptoms, treatment, and diagnosis. C.D.C also discusses ADHD in children and the resources children need to succeed at school and at home. Centers for Disease Control and Prevention also supports people and communities that are fighting diseases.

- ADHD World Federation
    - This resource promotes scientific and clinical study projects in ADHD and there is exchanging of information within the ADHD community.

- National Resource Center on Attention Deficit Hyperactivity Disorder
    - The National Resource Center on ADHD runs a program catering to both

children and adults diagnosed with ADHD. The organization also has up-to-date information about ADHD and guarantees that individuals receive enough information on the condition.

- American Psychological Association

  o This non-profit organization is a group website that gives information on ADHD, addictions, anger, anxiety, bullying, medication, and other mental health issues. A psychologist in a specific area can be located with links that are found on the American Psychological Association website.

- ADHD CME Faculty

  o This resource provides valuable education about adult ADHD and is beneficial for both healthcare workers and members of the public. The organization even offers medical education with the goal of assisting doctors and other healthcare workers in the management and diagnosis of ADHD.

Blogs

Blogs are filled with useful information about attention deficit hyperactivity disorder. People who live with ADHD, write about their experience online. But these blogs must be checked by professionals of ADHD.

Online Communities

Local ADHD organizations and national organizations have social media accounts; the online communities offer a wealth of useful information and supportive resources. Online communities include:

- Reddit
    - This web resource provides users with information pertaining to ADHD. Individuals suffering with the problem can find support and community through talking to others about personal experiences with ADHD. Individuals may share their challenges and the non-medication techniques that have helped them. If you try this online platform, you can also have access to the weekly positivity threads.

- Facebook
    - Facebook is one of the most popular social media which is accessible by almost everyone. This social media platform allows individuals with ADHD to connect with others who live with ADHD. Not all Facebook groups are accessible, an individual needs a request to join because some are strictly private.

- podcasts
    - There are various podcasts discussing life with ADHD. Some information might not be correct, so individuals

must search for verified accounts, many organizations have a specific symbol indicating that they are real. The following are some of the expert-hosted podcasts:

- ADHD 365 and All things ADHD

  - are two podcasts for Children and Adults with Attention Deficit Hyperactivity Disorder (CHADD) that address different ADHD-related topics for individuals with ADHD.

- ADDitude's ADHD Expert Podcast

  - This podcast records question-and-answer webinars that have information from experts who want to share their knowledge on the condition.

- ADHD reWired

  - The mind behind this podcast is called Eric Tivers, a psychotherapist who is also an author. He also has ADHD and teaches about his experience with ADHD apart from giving general information about ADHD.

- ■ Hacking your ADHD

  - This podcast teaches different techniques that help individuals with ADHD. William Curb runs the podcast and calls himself the proud "owner of an attention deficit hyperactivity disorder brain."

Books

Resources for ADHD can also be found in different books, some of the books recorded as audiobooks or audio CDs which is beneficial to individuals who find reading as a challenge. The following are some of the books:

- *A Radical Guide Women with ADHD: Embrace Neurodiversity, Live Boldly, and Break Through Barriers*

  - This gem helps ladies who suffer from ADHD by empowering them to soar above shame-based narratives and negative self-talk. The three genius authors who put the book together are:

Ellen Litman, Sari Solden, and Michelle Frank.

- *The Adult ADHD Toolkit*

  ○ This one was written by two people, namely J. Russell Ramsay, Ph.D. and Anthony L. Rostain, M.D. It is a kit filled with explanations about strategies which help with planning, emotional challenge, procrastination and motivation. Tips are given to guide individuals with ADHD with their personal struggles.

- *Smart but Stuck*

  ○ This ADHD treasure was crafted by Thomas E. Brown, Ph.D. It covers the several ways in which ADHD may manifest in different areas of an individual's life. It explains how symptoms impact emotions and how ADHD mostly co-occurs with other mental health disorders like mood and anxiety disorders.

- *Driven to Distraction* and *Delivered from Distraction*

  ○ These are highly recommended books since individuals with ADHD are easily distracted and lose focus and end up losing their jobs written by Edward M. Hallowell, M.D., and John J. Ratey, M.D. It explains a specific unique list of attention deficit hyperactivity disorder manifestations.

Chapter 12:

List of Common ADHD

Medications

Generic Name	Brand(s)	Common Side Effects	Precautions
Amphetamine and Dextroamphetamine	Adderall XR, Mydayis	Fast beating heart, headache, nervousness	Not to be taken in larger doses, take as prescribed by your physician. Contact the emergency line if you experience serious side effects like hallucinations, depression, or numbness.
Amphetamine	Adzenys XR,	Dry mouth, diarrhea,	Do not take larger doses

	Adzenys ER, Dyanavel XR	nervousness, change in libido	than prescribed and take it often as your physician instructed. Notify your doctor if you have any cardiovascular diseases
Atomoxetine	Strattera	Diarrhea, dry mouth, or insomnia	It is not recommended in people who have cardiac diseases like hypertension, or atrial fibrillation. Contact your physician if you get suicide ideations as well.
Alpha2 agonists	Clonidine and Guanfacine	Decreased heart rate, sudden drop in blood pressure, and dry mouth	It is not recommended in people suffering from liver disease and kidney disease. Rebound

			hypertension can occur if you suddenly stop taking the medication
Bupropion	Wellbutrin and Zyban	Headache, anxiety, and dry mouth	Not recommended in people living with a seizure disorder as it can trigger seizures in these individuals.
Dexmethylphenidate	Focalin	Appetite loss, dry mouth, insomnia, fatigue	It is not recommended in people using MAOIs antidepressants and in those with cardiovascular diseases.
Dexmethylphenidate and Serdexmethylphenidate	Azstarys	Nausea, vomiting, indigestion, insomnia	Before taking the medication inform your physician if you have hypertension, any heart

			problems or mental health problems.
Dextroamphetamine	Dexedrine, Dextrostat	Dry mouth, increased heart rate, abdominal pain	It is not recommended if one has a history of substance abuse, and in those with cardiovascular diseases.
Lisdexamfetamine	Vyvanse	Nausea, vomiting, nervousness	Not recommended to people who have hypertension, those sensitive to amphetamine
Methamphetamine	Desoxyn, Methedrine	Increased heart rate, excessive sweating, diarrhea, loss of appetite	Not recommended if you are hypertensive to other stimulant drugs, if you have cardiovascular diseases, or have a history

			of using recreational drugs.
Guanfacine ER	Tenex	Irritability, fatigue	Contraindicated in people who are hypertensive to guanfacine.
Methylphenidate, Methylphenidate ER	Concerta, Adhansia XR, Aptensio XR	Increased heart rate, anxiety, and raised high blood pressure	Can cause a painful prolonged erection, medicine should not be stopped suddenly.
Viloxazine	Qelbree	Insomnia, headache, and increased blood pressure	This drug is not recommended for use if you have kidney disease or are hypertensive.

Conclusion

Conclusion

As promised, we have explored answers to eleven key questions about adult ADHD. My hope is that this book gives you and your loved ones the strength to go forward knowing you have control over the condition.

It is crucial that you take the information in this guide as friendly advice, not treatment options for yourself, friends, or family members living with ADHD. My objective is to arm you with the proper knowledge for informed decision-making when living with adult ADHD. When you need recommendations about medication, always remember to contact your local physician, pharmacist, or mental health expert.

If you know someone else living with adult ADHD or one whose loved one has it, you might want to spread some knowledge. Feel free to recommend this manual to them if you found it informative.

References

ADDitude Editors. (2006, October 6). *ADHD statistics.*
ADDitude.
https://www.additudemag.com/statistics-of-adhd/

ADHD medications and alcohol interactions. (n.d.).
Drugs.com.
https://www.drugs.com/article/adhd-medication-alcohol.html

Arnsten, A. F. T. (2009). ADHD and the prefrontal
cortex. *The Journal of Pediatrics, 154*(5), I-S43.
https://doi.org/10.1016/j.jpeds.2009.01.018

Austin, R., & Pisano, G. (2017, July 18). *Neurodiversity is
a competitive advantage.* Harvard Business Review.
https://hbr.org/2017/05/neurodiversity-as-a-competitive-advantage

Barkla, X. M., McArdle, P. A., & Newbury-Birch, D.
(2015). Are there any potentially dangerous
pharmacological effects of combining ADHD
medication with alcohol and drugs of abuse? A
systematic review of the literature. *BMC
Psychiatry, 15*, 270.
https://doi.org/10.1186/s12888-015-0657-9

Brenis, J. (2017a, December 8). *Duane Gordon, creative genius, and ADHD hero.* Adhdatwork. https://adhdatwork.add.org/duane-gordon-creative-genius-and-adhd-hero

Brenis, J. (2017b, December 8). *Jay Carter: When employers invest in ADHD employees.* Adhdatwork. https://adhdatwork.add.org/jay-carter-when-employers-invest-in-adhd-employees/

Centers for Disease Control and Prevention. (2018a). *Symptoms and diagnosis of ADHD.* Centers for Disease Control and Prevention. https://www.cdc.gov/ncbddd/adhd/diagnosis.html

Centers for Disease Control and Prevention. (2018b). *Treatment of ADHD.* Centers for Disease Control and Prevention. https://www.cdc.gov/ncbddd/adhd/treatment.html

Centers for Disease Control and Prevention. (2021, September 23). *What is ADHD?* Centers for Disease Control and Prevention. https://www.cdc.gov/ncbddd/adhd/facts.html

Cherry, K. (2022, March 22). *Why ADHD is often untreated in adults.* Verywell Mind. https://www.verywellmind.com/untreated-adhd-in-adults-signs-causes-impact-and-treatment-5222929

Chou, C.-C., & Huang, C.-J. (2017). *Effects of an 8-week yoga program on sustained attention and discrimination function in children with attention deficit hyperactivity disorder.* PeerJ, 5, e2883. https://doi.org/10.7717/peerj.2883

Chung, W., Jiang, S.-F., Paksarian, D., Nikolaidis, A., Castellanos, F. X., Merikangas, K. R., & Milham, M. P. (2019). Trends in the prevalence and incidence of attention-deficit/hyperactivity disorder among adults and children of different racial and ethnic groups. *JAMA Network Open, 2*(11), e1914344. https://doi.org/10.1001/jamanetworkopen.201 9.14344

Corbisiero, S., Bitto, H., Newark, P., Abt-Mörstedt, B., Elsässer, M., Buchli-Kammermann, J., Künne, S., Nyberg, E., Hofecker-Fallahpour, M., & Stieglitz, R.-D. (2018). A Comparison of Cognitive-Behavioral Therapy and Pharmacotherapy vs. Pharmacotherapy Alone in Adults with Attention-Deficit/Hyperactivity Disorder (ADHD)—A Randomized Controlled Trial. *Frontiers in Psychiatry, 9.* https://doi.org/10.3389/fpsyt.2018.00571

Corrigendum to sluggish cognitive tempo, internalizing symptoms, and executive function in adults with ADHD. (2020). *Journal of Attention Disorders, 24*(10), 1472–1472. https://doi.org/10.1177/1087054720927868

Den Heijer, A. E., Groen, Y., Tucha, L., Fuermaier, A. B. M., Koerts, J., Lange, K. W., Thome, J., & Tucha, O. (2016). Sweat it out? The effects of physical exercise on cognition and behavior in children and adults with ADHD: a systematic literature review. *Journal of Neural Transmission, 124*(S1), 3–26. https://doi.org/10.1007/s00702-016-1593-7

Dowd, K. E. (2017, April 28). *Michael Phelps opens up about ADHD struggles*. Sports Illustrated. https://www.si.com/olympics/2017/04/28/michael-phelps-opens-about-adhd-struggles-teacher-told-me-id-never-amount-anything

Fayyad, J., Sampson, N. A., Hwang, I., Adamowski, T., Aguilar-Gaxiola, S., Al-Hamzawi, A., Andrade, L. H. S. G., Borges, G., de Girolamo, G., Florescu, S., Gureje, O., Haro, J. M., Hu, C., Karam, E. G., Lee, S., Navarro-Mateu, F., O'Neill, S., Pennell, B.-E., Piazza, M., & Posada-Villa, J. (2016). The descriptive epidemiology of DSM-IV adult ADHD in the world health organization world mental health surveys. *ADHD Attention Deficit and Hyperactivity Disorders, 9*(1), 47–65. https://doi.org/10.1007/s12402-016-0208-3

Geffen, J., & Forster, K. (2017). Treatment of adult ADHD: A clinical perspective. *Therapeutic Advances in Psychopharmacology, 8*(1), 25–32. https://doi.org/10.1177/2045125317734977

Israel, J. A. (2015). *Combining stimulants and monoamine oxidase inhibitors: A reexamination of the literature and a report of a new treatment combination*. The Primary Care Companion for CNS Disorders. https://doi.org/10.4088/pcc.15br01836

Katzman, M. A., Bilkey, T. S., Chokka, P. R., Fallu, A., & Klassen, L. J. (2017). Adult ADHD and comorbid disorders: Clinical implications of a dimensional approach. *BMC Psychiatry, 17*(1). https://doi.org/10.1186/s12888-017-1463-3

Kooij, S. (2013). *Adult ADHD diagnostic assessment and treatment.* London Springer.

Kronenberg, L. M., Goossens, P. J. J., van Busschbach, J., van Achterberg, T., & van den Brink, W. (2015). Coping styles in substance use disorder (SUD) patients with and without co-occurring attention deficit/hyperactivity disorder (ADHD) or autism spectrum disorder (ASD). *BMC Psychiatry, 15*(1). https://doi.org/10.1186/s12888-015-0530-x

Managing ADHD in children, adolescents, and adults with comorbid anxiety in primary care. (2007). *Primary Care Companion to the Journal of Clinical Psychiatry, 9*(2), 129–138. https://www.ncbi.nlm.nih.gov/pmc/articles/PMC1896299/

Medication chart to treat attention deficit disorders. (n.d.). ADD WareHouse. https://www.addwarehouse.com/article3.htm

Mehren, A., Reichert, M., Coghill, D., Müller, H. H. O., Braun, N., & Philipsen, A. (2020). Physical exercise in attention deficit hyperactivity disorder – evidence and implications for the treatment of borderline personality disorder. *Borderline Personality Disorder and Emotion*

Dysregulation, 7(1). https://doi.org/10.1186/s40479-019-0115-2

National Institute of Mental Health. (n.d.). *Attention-Deficit/hyperactivity disorder (ADHD)*. Nimh. https://www.nimh.nih.gov/health/statistics/attention-deficit-hyperactivity-disorder-adhd

Nimmo-Smith, V., Merwood, A., Hank, D., Brandling, J., Greenwood, R., Skinner, L., Law, S., Patel, V., & Rai, D. (2020). Non-pharmacological interventions for adult ADHD: a systematic review. *Psychological Medicine,* 50(4), 1–13. https://doi.org/10.1017/s0033291720000069

Pfiffner, L. J., & Haack, L. M. (2014). Behavior management for school-aged children with ADHD. *Child and Adolescent Psychiatric Clinics of North America,* 23(4), 731–746. https://doi.org/10.1016/j.chc.2014.05.014

Quinn, P. O., & Madhoo, M. (2014). A review of attention-deficit/hyperactivity disorder in women and girls. *The Primary Care Companion for CNS Disorders,* 16(3). https://doi.org/10.4088/pcc.13r01596

Rosario-Hernández, E., & Rovira-Millán, L. (2020). ADHD and its effects on job performance: A moderated mediation model. *Spring,* 4(1), 1–25. https://doi.org/10.37226/rcp.2020/01

Silva, A. P., Prado, S. O. S., Scardovelli, T. A., Boschi, S. R. M. S., Campos, L. C., & Frère, A. F. (2015). Measurement of the effect of physical exercise on the concentration of individuals with ADHD. *PLOS ONE, 10*(3), e0122119. https://doi.org/10.1371/journal.pone.0122119

Sprich, S. E., Safren, S. A., Finkelstein, D., Remmert, J. E., & Hammerness, P. (2016). A randomized controlled trial of cognitive behavioral therapy for ADHD in medication-treated adolescents. *Journal of Child Psychology and Psychiatry, 57*(11), 1218–1226. https://doi.org/10.1111/jcpp.12549

The Understood Team. (n.d.). *Why Lisa Ling was relieved by her ADHD diagnosis.* Understood. https://www.understood.org/en/articles/celeb rity-spotlight-why-journalist-lisa-ling-was-relieved-by-her-adhd-diagnosis?_sp=f7e54812-de5f-4848-b3b3-7ed5509171ee.1665496698957

Tistarelli, N., Fagnani, C., Troianiello, M., Stazi, M. A., & Adriani, W. (2020). The nature and nurture of ADHD and its comorbidities: A narrative review on twin studies. *Neuroscience & Biobehavioral Reviews, 109*(109), 63–77. https://doi.org/10.1016/j.neubiorev.2019.12.01 7

WebMD Editorial Contributors. (2008, October 17). *ADHD organizations.* WebMD. https://www.webmd.com/add-adhd/childhood-adhd/adhd-resources

Wegrzyn, S. C., Hearrington, D., Martin, T., & Randolph, A. B. (2012). Brain games as a potential nonpharmaceutical alternative for the treatment of ADHD. *Journal of Research on Technology in Education, 45*(2), 107–130. https://doi.org/10.1080/15391523.2012.10782599

Weiss, M., Murray, C., Wasdell, M., Greenfield, B., Giles, L., & Hechtman, L. (2012). A randomized controlled trial of CBT therapy for adults with ADHD with and without medication. *BMC Psychiatry, 12*(1). https://doi.org/10.1186/1471-244x-12-30

Weiss, M., & Weiss, J. (2004). A guide to the treatment of adults with ADHD A guide to the treatment of adults with ADHD. *J Clin Psychiatry, 65*(3). https://www.psychiatrist.com/wp-content/uploads/2021/02/13791_guide-treatment-adults-adhd.pdf

Wilkins, B. (2021, October 6). *Jamie Oliver tells a moving story of coping with learning difficulties.* HELLO! https://www.hellomagazine.com/healthandbeauty/health-and-fitness/20211006123352/jamie-oliver-dyslexic-adhd-video/

Made in United States
Orlando, FL
08 December 2023

40494341R00108